JAVA STYLE

◆

Photographer's Dedication

To my parents: my mother, Sribadi Chususiah, and to the memory of my father, Sumaryo Sosrowardoyo, who was never to know that I would act on the passion for light and shadow that he'd instilled in me.

And to Haga Tara Sosrowardoyo, because I love him more than he will ever be able to imagine; and to Ina, for all the best reasons.

Tara Sosrowardoyo

◆

Editorial Director	**Timothy Auger**
Editor	**Tim Jaycock**
Photo Editor	**Marie-Claude Millet**
Designer	**Nelani Jinadasa**
Production Manager	**Edmund Lam**
Artwork	**Atang F., Ujang Suherman**

◆

Acknowledgments

The publishers would like to thank the owners and proprietors of each and every building photographed in this book.

Special thanks to Ratina Moegiono for her style and expert co-ordination. Thanks also to the photographer's team: Sidup Damiri, Tony Tjahjono, Tantyo Bangun, Haga Tara, Reita Malaon and Doddy Mukhaesin.

The publishers are grateful to the Office of the Governor of Jakarta, for permission to use the illustration on page 76, to Yusman Siswandi, Jaya Ibrahim, K.R.T. Hardjonegoro, Gallery 59 and Mr. and Mrs. Anhar Setjadibrata of the Tugu Park Hotel in Malang.

◆

Illustration credits

All photographs were taken by Tara Sosrowardoyo, except those on:
endpapers: PhotoBank
pages 15 (top) and 17: from *Het Paradijs van Java*, Wijnand Kerkhoff, Amsterdam [undated]
pages 15 and 37: from *Java. Beelden van volksleven en bedrijf*, Emilie van Kerckhoff, Scheltema & Holkema: Amsterdam c.1912
page 20, 72, 74: from *Nederlandsch Oost-Indie Typen*, Auguste van Pers, J.C. van Schenk Brill: The Hague 1853–62
page 26: Brent Hesselyn collection, photographed by Rio Helmi; except iv, vi, xi, EDM private collection
page 36: artwork by Anuar bin Abdul Rahim — insets after *Rumah Tradisionil Jawa*, Drs. Hamzuri, Departemen Pendidikan dan Kebudayaan, Jakarta [undated]; main picture based on a drawing by Gunawan Tjahjono in *Cosmos, Center, and Duality in Javanese Architectural Tradition*, PhD dissertation, University of California: Berkeley 1989
page 38: from *Oud Batavia Platen Album*, G. Kolff & Co.: Batavia [sic] 1923
page 73: J.C. Rappard, from *Nederlandsche-Indie*, vol. 3, *Java*, Van Rees: [place of publication not stated] 1883
page 76: Mindglow Design, from *Gedung Balai Kota Jakarta*, Jalan Merdeka Selatan No. 8, Pemerintah DKI Jakarta: Jakarta 1996
page 77: from *Tempo doeloe*, vol. *Komen en blijven*, Rob Nieuwenhuys, Em. Querido's Uitgeverij B.V.: Amsterdam 1982
page 105: from *Ir. F.J.L. Ghijselss, Architect in Indonesia [1910–1929]*, Drs. H. Akihary, Seram Press: Utrecht 1996

◆

This edition published in 1997 by Periplus Edition (HK) Ltd

Produced by Editions Didier Millet
593 Havelock Road #02-01,
Singapore 169641

◆

Text © Peter Schoppert 1997
Photographs © Tara Sosrowardoyo 1997
© Editions Didier Millet 1997

Colour separation by Colourscan
Printed by Tien Wah Press (Pte) Ltd

Printed and bound in Singapore

ISBN 962-593-232-1

JAVA STYLE

Photography by
TARA SOSROWARDOYO

Text by
PETER SCHOPPERT

With the collaboration of
SOEDARMADJI DAMAIS

PERIPLUS

EDITIONS

contents

orientation 12

the great tradition 30

tempo doeloe 70

modernisms 100

contemporary homes 140

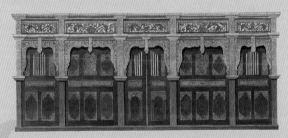

javanese design 198

suggested reading 207

index 208

Javanese archetypes: wooden columns rise to support a Javanese pendopo *or* pavilion, one which shelters a classical torso from Java's Hindu-Buddhist period. The aesthetic of the romantic past is not a Western import to Java; in the 14th century Majapahit nobles travelled to ruined temples and bathing pools surrounded by jungle to enjoy the evocative atmosphere.

Following pages: Javanese schoolgirls cycle past the towering silhouettes of the Prambanan temple complex. Consecrated a thousand years ago, the temple tells in its reliefs the ancient epic of the Ramayana. Java is a youthful society, but one graced with the reminder of a glorious past.

"Waving forests, never-failing streams and constant verdure": this was the landscape of Java in the eyes of colonial administrator Sir Stamford Raffles. Java's greenness is matched only by the density of its population. Even its cities are green: scholars are intrigued by the Javanese style of urbanism, with neighbourhoods organized on village lines, with communally shared resources. Greenery, including fruit trees and ornamentals, are crammed into any available land.

◆

orient

ation

orientation

The 'style' that books of this sort deal with is above all about sense of place, the feeling for a location that comes from its architecture and landscape, from interiors, views and vistas both intimate and panoramic, furniture and fittings, the domestic settings for the mundane moments that

Mt. Merapi rises to the north of the temple complex of Prambanan. The siting of Javanese temples rivals Greece; and the continuity of old ideas of orientation is most striking.

make up a way of life. The aim of such books is to sketch out what is particular—in visual terms—about a city, region, island or nation.

Attempting to do the same for the island of Java is a rash undertaking (as the reader will come to appreciate soon enough). This is an island of 120 million people, a complex and sophisticated society in the midst of wrenching changes. Here is Jakarta, with the brashest high-rises in all of *nouveau-riche* Asia, with traffic jams on the epic scale, where yuppies wielding hand phones like pistols eat *sushi* in super-luxe hotels kitted out with marble, piped-in bird song and two hundred-year-old woodcarvings. Here is Solo, a stately court city where the Susuhunan dons his coat of many colours and his welded-steel *keris* to perform solemn rituals, to preserve what is left of the cosmic order. The younger scions of his noble court, arrayed in formal Javanese

batik skirts and high-collared velvet tunics, capture the proceedings on their video cameras. Here are the villages of the Badui, who have for centuries deliberately rejected novel ways and ideas, farming the old rice varieties, doing without electricity, chemical fertilizer or diesel fuel, and worshipping deities who have Hindu names but the ancestors' features. When the rice is harvested, some will walk the hundred and fifty miles to Jakarta to sell their handmade twine bags on the crowded pavements.

In the two thousand years of its recorded history, Java has encountered all the civilizations of Euro-Asia, and has taken, borrowed, purchased or inherited from them what it has needed or desired. Almost every world religion is here in force: Islam, puritan, orthodox and mystical, Christianity both Catholic and Protestant, Hinduism in all its unruly variation, Buddhism of the larger and lesser vehicle, the moral philosophy of Confucius and the old practices of ancestor worship and propitiation of the Thunder God. This openness leads most observers to try and reduce Java to a sum of influences, from India, China, Arabia, or Europe. Rabindranath Tagore tried that too but could not complete the equation: "I see India everywhere but I do not recognize it."

Java remains utterly Java. And no matter how confusing the cultural landscape, how rich the mix, how many bends in the road, the Javanese remain oriented. "Walk a hundred meters to the north, then head east". "Leave by the western door". In the Javanese heartland, one navigates using the cardinal directions. Someone who is hopelessly confused is said to be unable to recognize true north. The symbolism of the directions, four plus one, permeates Javanese thought: east, south, west, north and centre. The great ancient monument of Borobudur is oriented two-and-a-half degrees off magnetic compass readings, with ranks of

This shows a traditional Sundanese house, raised off the ground, with a curved roof ridge and crossed gable ends.

Buddha statues facing outward to each of the cardinal directions, a *stupa* at their centre. Borobudur's eastern face confronts a sun that rises over the peak of a great volcano, 'the fiery one', Mt. Merapi. Jalan Malioboro, the main road of Yogyakarta in Central Java runs due north from the gates of the palace of the sultan, across the perpendicular railroad tracks, to point directly at Merapi's imposing peak. Everything, including the volcanos, is related on a cosmic grid.

And that grid is centred upon a small hill in Central Java outside of Magelang: the Tidar, a point very near the exact geographical centre of the island, as measured on modern maps. It is—so the legend goes—the head of the nail that holds Java to the earth. Is there a stronger basis for a sense of place than that?

The materials of the tropical environment are the foundations of Java Style. Bamboo is among the most versatile of these, as can be seen in the village gateway in this early-20th-century print.

Java anchors the gentle arc of islands that makes up the *nusantara,* the great Southeast-Asian archipelago. The island is long, narrow and volcanic, some 650 miles in length but only 120 miles wide at its widest point, and lies roughly parallel and six degrees south of the equator. Its northern coast fronts on the shallow, welcoming Java Sea, and its southern coast confronts the depths of the Java Trench and the Indian Ocean, or as they say in Java, the *Laut Kidul,* the Southern Ocean. Java has been a home for man for a million-and-a-half years, and is today the heart of the Republic of Indonesia, its 120 million people forming some 60% of the Republic's young population, while taking up only 7% of the nation's total land area.

That such a small island (smaller than Great Britain) can support so many, and on what is still a largely agricultural base, is a testament to Java's immense natural wealth. Its 30 volcanoes bring nutrients to the soil of the broad central and eastern plains, while their peaks capture rain, redistributing it as run-off.

"Java is singularly favoured in the number of its streams." So said Sir Stamford Raffles, son of the Enlightenment and ruler over Java for the few brief years of the British interregnum in the early 19th century. He was frankly enamoured of Java's landscape, writing that it "may be reckoned amongst the most romantic and highly diversified in the world; uniting all the rich and magnificent scenery, which waving forests, never-failing streams and constant verdure can present, heightened by a pure atmosphere and the glowing tints of a tropical sun."

Javanese villages, towns and even cities are generally green places. Raffles was struck by the greenery of Javanese villages "so completely screened from the rays of a scorching sun, and so buried amid the foliage of a luxuriant vegetation". Nearly two hundred years later, V.S. Naipaul was equally impressed with the "yards full of shade and fruit and flowers".

The tropical climate is of course a central element shaping the forms of Java Style, i.e. housing and furnishings. The equatorial heat is tempered by the surrounding seas, and the thermometer rarely breaks 95° Fahrenheit or 35° Centigrade. Temperatures usually range between 77° and 90° in the daytime, falling a mere six or seven degrees at night. Humidity is high, so the climate is unkind to perishable materials. The island is mountainous, and temperatures fall quickly on the slopes of the volcanoes. On the highest peaks, near-freezing temperatures have been reported.

Subject to the southern cycle of monsoon winds,

In Java, pyramidal roofs like this one are reserved for holy buildings, usually for mosques. Varied roof shapes, an important Austronesian heritage, can be seen in the print below.

Java enjoys distinct dry and wet seasons, but as Sir Stamford observed, it is very well-watered all year round, some areas receiving as much rain as any place in the world. In sum, Java's climate and its natural setting strike nearly everyone who ponders such things as being uniquely conducive to the flourishing of man.

The precise importance of Java in the unique tale of man's origins is uncertain. Java's *Homo erectus* remains —the famous Java Man—date back some one-and-a-half million years, and are among the oldest outside Africa. But the relationship between those early humans and later *Homo sapiens* is a mystery.

What is certain is that today's Javanese are descended from much more recent arrivals to the island. Their ancestors were Austronesian-speaking peoples who came to the island some five thousand years ago. The exact dynamics of trade and cultural exchange, movements of ideas and the movements of populations will probably never be precisely unravelled, but it is clear that Austronesian peoples and Austronesian ways followed an island-hopping path from what is now Southern China, to Taiwan and then the Philippines, then southward through Sulawesi to Java and the rest of Indonesia. The Austronesian migrations brought to Java a particular agricultural tool kit, including the cultivation of rice, and an architectural and design heritage that remains legible today. And the Austronesians found in Java a place well suited to their own ways of life.

Diversity was built into the Austronesian pattern of life from the start, as the myriad niches of the *nusantara* ecology encouraged various and interdependent economies and societies. As with most of Southeast Asia, Java's population today is far from homogeneous, with two generally recognized indigenous ethnic groups inhabiting the island, the Javanese and

Sundanese, together with a third from the island of Madura just off Java's northeastern corner, the Madurese. Various indigenous subgroups maintain a distinct identity in remote valleys and on mountain plateaux, and a cosmopolitan variety of comparatively recent arrivals is concentrated in the cities and towns.

The majority Javanese are mostly lowland dwellers, farming in the broad plains around the slopes of the volcanic mountains of the central and eastern portions of the island. The centre of the Javanese areas is the *nagarigung*, and it comprises the fertile crescent around Mt. Merapi, including the two old court cities of Yogyakarta and Solo or Surakarta. There is a western periphery, the *monconegari kulon,* which comprises the plains around Banyumas, and an eastern one: the *monconegari wetan*, the rice-growing plains of today's East Java province, areas drained by the Brantas River.

A broad, gentle, fertile coastal plain forms the North Coast region of the island, but in the western interior the volcanoes are close together, creating a higher, more rugged landscape not so suited to irrigated rice. This region is home to the Sundanese, by tradition dry-land farmers. The Sundanese and Javanese speak different languages, and are culturally quite distinct. Though they share much in art and ways of life, the Sundanese have never had the all-embracing court culture of Central Java.

In the east, and just off the North Coast of Java, is the island of Madura. The limestone island is drier and poorer than Java, and so the Madurese are more likely to be fishermen and traders than rice farmers. In the past they were famed as warriors and mercenaries, and for centuries they have sought their fortune outside their home island. In the early part of this century, many Madurese migrated to the 'far east' of Java, the eastern salient that runs from Malang to the Gilamanuk Straits facing Bali. They now dominate the region.

This religious school in West Java illustrates some of the basic principles of Javanese house construction, with its wooden and woven bamboo walls and a double-beam roof truss. The floor is covered by split bamboo mats, perhaps the ultimate solution for providing a smooth cool surface for sitting and standing.

The North Coast of Java, a broad coastal plain running from Banten in the west to Gresik and Surabaya in the east, makes up a distinct cultural zone called the Pasisir, though its people generally identify themselves as ethnically Javanese (with some exceptions in the western portion of the zone). The Pasisir is linked by the gentle, shallow Java Sea to the coastal areas of Sumatra, Borneo, the Malay Peninsula and Sulawesi. Linked by the sea, not separated, for the North Coast has always been Java's opening to the world, a highly cosmopolitan place where the peoples and cultures of Asia and indeed the world have met. Few places give a better visual expression to the longevity of the competition and mutual enrichment of cultures, colours and ideas than the North Coast of Java, with its lively *batik,* and its palaces and mosques redolent of Southeast Asia's great trading age in the 15th and 16th centuries.

Neoclassical architecture was an important influence on Java's sense of design and proportion. The columns of this tomb complex in Madura are fine examples.

The Betawi or Batavians of Jakarta are a cultural group that arose from the Pasisir way of life. They are the children of Java's largest city, Indonesia's capital, Jakarta, which has a five-hundred-year history as a metropolis and meeting point. Here various Indonesian peoples formed a distinct ethnic group in the melting pot of the colonial capital then known as Batavia. Speaking a form of Malay, with an architecture which is a heady mix of Buginese, Balinese, Chinese, Dutch and other traditions, the Orang Betawi have contributed much to what it means to be Indonesian. As a distinct group they are becoming swamped in the human tides of Jakarta—with twelve million inhabitants it is among the world's most populous cities—but their food and dialect are at the heart of the city's life.

One must add to the ethnic map sketched above various isolated groups like the Baduy, who work hard to maintain ethnic identities distinct from the masses around them. Crucial to the overall picture are the Chinese, whose history as sojourners and settlers in Java dates back many centuries. Added too must be peoples from the Arabian peninsula and the Indian Subcontinent, the Indos or Eurasian cultural group, and more recently the many non-Javanese who have settled here from original homes all over the Indonesian republic. That sketchy map outlines a story of tremendous human diversity and a cosmopolitan way of life. It is a rich setting, indeed, for Java Style.

The prehistoric Austronesian peoples of the *nusantara* had four great skills: as seafarers, as rice growers, as textile makers, and as architects. Five thousand years on, the peoples of Java are still worthy of this inheritance.

The Austronesian expansion was the first and greatest Age of Exploration, as Austronesians traversed the island arc of Asia, and then eastwards across the vastness of the Pacific Ocean, travelling as far (at least) as Hawaii, New Zealand and Easter Island. Their voyages westward brought them to India, Arabia and beyond. The Austronesian languages spoken on Madagascar, off the coast of Southern Africa, are thought by scholars to be related to Javanese and languages from Borneo. The 9th-century-CE temple reliefs on Central Java's Borobudur temple portray large, ocean-going ships of Southeast-Asian design, filled with traders and pilgrims going to and returning from far-off lands. In the 16th century the Portuguese were delighted to have captured a Javanese map that clearly portrayed Europe and Brazil, as well as coastal Asia. Java's mastery of the seas ended in the 17th century, but its engagement in trade and the affairs of Asia and the world remain.

As farmers, the people of Java perfected wet-rice cultivation. Rice thrives in swamps and wetlands, and the discovery that rice grew best in waterlogged fields must have been part of the knowledge base of the Austronesians at an early date, perhaps as long as seven thousand years ago. Still, the gentle, curving slopes of the volcanoes of Java and Bali are perfectly suited to the establishment of irrigation systems, and it is in these soils wet rice cultivation reached its peak.

Contrary to early theories, it seems that successful irrigation systems require no central control, no 'oriental despot' to commandeer labour, and to plan great canals. Networks of villages can create and maintain irrigation systems of great complexity and effectiveness, with the right cultural tools for mediating conflicts. Such irrigation systems created the rice surpluses that supported the classical age of Javanese civilization, and made Java famous for its rice exports a thousand years ago. Despite the changes brought by new agricultural methods and land pressures, such systems still thrive on Bali, and in parts of Java, such as on the slopes of Mt. Lawu near Solo.

Throughout central and eastern Java, and in parts of the west, rice terracing on hill slopes means farmers can make full use of scarce land. Terraces are prepared for the rice by ploughing, the soil breaking down into an impermeable mud which helps hold the water of the flooded bunds. Rice seeds are planted in special plots, where they are attended with obsessive care. When the seedlings have grown, they are transplanted to flooded terraces. The panorama of flooded fields, their surfaces reflecting the thunderheads of wet-season skies soon gives way to the incredible viridity of young rice plants. At harvest time, the rice stalks droop with the weight of the golden heads of rice. Rice terraces transform the dramatic Javanese earth into a domestic realm, transposing the volcanic landscape to a human scale. This transformation is an essential element in the total experience of Java Style.

The Indo-European house deploys ornament of European houses in a form that is Javanese: with its veranda, characteristic roof shape, and longitudinal organization of space.

With rice so dominant in the Javanese life and landscape, is it any wonder that it is traditionally viewed as something sacred? Dewi Sri is the goddess of rice and fertility. Older Javanese homes preserve a shrine to her in the *senthong,* a small room in the innermost portion of house. Her power ensures that in some areas the ripened rice is still harvested with a tiny hand knife, the *ani-ani,* rather than with a sickle. Harvesting with an *ani-ani* is slow and inefficient, as each stalk is severed singly. But it is also humble and respectful, an almost apologetic means of gathering the harvest of the deity of the rice fields.

In the days of high colonialism, life was lived on the cool veranda: the semi-public place where governors met with the governed.

As textile-makers, the Austronesians mastered the art of growing, spinning and weaving cotton, using a range of dyeing techniques to colour and pattern. Weavers are depicted in prehistoric bronzes, using the back-strap loom. Such looms are still seen in the more traditional parts of Java. But the old textile heritage has its greatest expression on Java today in the dominance of *batik,* a wax-resist method of colouring finished cloths. Though Javanese *batik* in the courts and on the North Coast has achieved a rare sophistication, it is still linked—through design motifs, dyestuffs and ritual—to the ancient textile tradition.

And as architects, the Austronesians were masters of the materials afforded in tropical and subtropical environments: wood, bamboo, rattans, grasses and the products of the many varieties of palm tree. Making a most elegant use of these natural materials, the Austronesian house is characterized first and foremost by its roof. Supported by thick wooden columns which convey its load directly to the ground, the roof is the dominant element. Living space is typically formed by a wooden platform or raft, which is attached to the columns, and raised from the ground.

Walls in an Austronesian house are optional. At any rate, they bear no load. In Java, this is clearly seen today in the most characteristic feature of local architecture, the *pendopo.* The *pendopo,* a variant of the old Sanskrit word *mandapa* or hall, is a kind of large pavilion built on columns. Square or rectangular in plan, the *pendopo* is open on all sides, providing shelter from direct sun and rain, but welcoming breezes and indirect light. Multatuli's explanation in the great colonial reformist novel *Max Havelaar* is suitably pithy: "next to a broad-rimmed hat, an umbrella or a hollow tree, a *pendoppo* is undoubtedly the simplest representation there is of the concept 'roof'." In Java today, *pendopos* are ritual spaces meant in the first place for ceremonies, but also used for receiving guests, and as a work space for cottage industry.

While the *pendopo* is an expression of an ancient element in Javanese architecture, in another important respect Java has turned out to be the exception to the Austronesian rule. Unlike the traditional houses in Sumatra, Borneo and Eastern Indonesia, almost all surviving Javanese homes have their floors built up from the ground. The fashion seems to have started in the cities of East Java in the 13th and 14th centuries, and spread throughout the island over the next five hundred years. By the end of the 19th century, Sundanese houses still included flexed roof ridges and floors raised from the ground, but today, a hundred years later, there are literally just a handful of such houses left in West Java, and a few rice barns on short piles in remote parts of East Java.

At the dawn of our era, and true to their Austronesian roots, the Javanese were trading through the region and across the Indian ocean. The ancient Indian epic the *Ramayana* describes Yavardvipa, an island rich in grain and gold, a reference that probably dates back to the 3rd century BCE. Grave finds of gold jewellery confirm such references.

In the 5th century CE an inscription in the *Pallava* script of Southern India turns up from King Puranavarman, ruler of the river valleys of northern West Java. Two centuries later the peoples of Central Java began to make inscriptions in Javanese using Indian lettering, and they began to make Hindu temples of stone and brick. The years 700 to, more or less, 920 CE saw a great flowering of art, scholarship and literature in Java. Monuments like Borobudur bear testament to the creative ferment taking place in this period: rice surpluses provided the wealth needed to create these temples, and priests, pilgrims and traders moved ideas and images in a lively exchange across the oceans, from India to Japan.

At the beginning of the 11th century, power shifted in Java from the central crescent around today's Yogyakarta and Solo, to the east, near the deltas of the Solo and Brantas rivers. Whether political crisis, volcanic eruption, epidemic or economic collapse, something seems to have disrupted the courts of Central Java, which only regained its seat as the centre of political power in the 16th century.

East Java offers a similar landscape to the central plains, with the added advantage of an easier

Songbirds are a staple of traditional Javanese life. Most popular is the Zebra dove or Perkutut. Doves with the best songs can command thousands of dollars, and recordings of dove songs are available commercially.

communication with the Java Sea. This plus a world trade boom from the 13th century until the end of the 16th, meant that Java became integrated into a trading network that was truly global. Foreign ways of life had a correspondingly higher impact. For example, at the end of the 13th century, Madurese armies turned back a Mongol expeditionary force. A hundred years later the Chinese were in East Java in force, helping to spread Islam, working the teak forests of Tuban to build ships in hybrid Chinese-Javanese styles, founding the port of Gresik, and building Chinese-type houses of masonry, with glazed roof tiles in exotic shapes.

The late 13th century saw the birth of the Majapahit kingdom, the Empire of the Bael or Golden Apple. It was to dominate the archipelago for the next one hundred and fifty years, commanding tribute from ports and principalities across the *nusantara*. The Majapahit Golden Age is commemorated in literature, most notably the *Nagarakertagama*, by holy man Mpu Prapanca, which describes a great capital of pavilions set in walled compounds. The earliest European visitor

Java's art and architecture of the 16th and 17th centuries witnesses a robust engagement between the new world of Islam and the Javanese Hindu-Buddhist past. Politically, Java had entered a time of deep uncertainty. No single court or city was able to dominate the island for the next two hundred years.

The new Kingdom of Mataram in Central Java, led by the Sultan Agung from 1613 to 1646, came closest. For a time it was challenged by Bantam, a Pasisir port wealthy on the pepper trade. Bantam first hosted small trading bases of those most recent arrivals, the Europeans. By the first quarter of the 17th century the dominant European presence was the Dutch Verenidge Oost-Indische Compagnie or VOC. Their military power, based on efficient weaponry and a fanatical courage, allowed them to challenge the military dominance of Mataram. The Dutch founded their capital Batavia on Bantam's doorstep in 1619, and over the next two hundred years they expanded through Java, first at the expense of the Pasisir, and later becoming drawn into conflicts with Central Javanese courts. This expansion was not a calculated operation: as Mataram lost central authority after the reign of Sultan Agung, the Dutch became drawn into internecine conflicts, concluding deals to control trade and taxes for cities or regions as the price for alliance.

In the end, the VOC was unable to cope with the demands of organization and administration of the territories in which it held power. The Company could not rein in the corruption that its officers thrived on, and bitter internal divisions had Batavia in a constant state of intrigue. Under the pressure of French and English competition for world trade, with revolution in Europe, the system collapsed, and the VOC was declared bankrupt. The very first day of the 19th century was the day that the sovereign French-Dutch government took over the administration of Java.

to Java, the intrepid Friar Odoric of Pordenone, was impressed, seemingly blind to but one element in the decor of the Majapahit capital: "The king of Java has a large and sumptuous palace, the most lofty of any that I have seen, with broad and lofty stairs to ascend to the upper apartments, all the steps being alternately of gold and silver. The whole interior walls are lined with plates of beaten gold, on which the images of warriors are placed sculpted in gold, having each a golden coronet richly ornamented with precious stones."

The Majapahit reign was a time of relative political unity across the archipelago, a unity that was later to inspire 20th-century nationalists as a model for an independent Indonesia. And importantly, Majapahit was witness to the coming of a new religion from the West. We know that members of the court adopted Islam. Majapahit's rulers never converted to Islam however, a religion which had first appeared in the region some two hundred years before. The first Islamic state on Java is Demak, one of the North Coast port cities. As internal conflicts weakened Majapahit, and as it lost trade to new ports like Malacca, on the eponymous Straits, Demak was able to challenge the old empire, succeeding over the last half of the 16th century.

The Dutch themselves had a new master in Napoleon. This affected Java in 1808, with the arrival of a new administrator in the Napoleonic style. Marshall Daendels set to with an energy foreign to the Company men, building a post road that linked Batavia to Bandung and Surabaya.

After the passage of three eventful years, another action man arrived in Java, together with a British army of occupation intent on denying Napoleon a strategic hold in Southeast Asia. Stamford Raffles ruled as Lieutenant-Governor for just a few short years, from 1811 to 1816. But his land reforms and intense curiosity about Java had an impact far beyond the brief years of his interregnum. His encyclopedic *History of Java* inaugurated intense scholarly interest in Java's archeological remains. The impact of this Enlightenment figure extends to furniture and design as well: the elegant neoclassical chair which is such a staple of Javanese interiors is known universally as 'the Raffles chair'.

Britain's interest in Java, and Raffles' land reforms, stimulated the Dutch régime to new efforts when they regained control in 1817, thanks to a European peace deal. In 1830 the Dutch introduced the Cultivation System, whereby peasants grew cash crops like coffee, sugar and indigo, for purchase by the state at its own prices. The system was to be a great financial success for the colony, making up an impressive 30% of Holland's total state revenue in the 1850s. At the same time, horrendous famines struck in Central Java.

The successful operation of the colony required the active co-operation of Javanese élites. Dutch government worked through local *bupati* or regents, who held all the trappings of power in their districts, and were themselves usually descended from families that had traditional claim to rule in the areas. The line of the kings of Mataram had split under pressure, but the Dutch were able to keep these splinter courts in a state of uneasy truce, now shoring up a weak ruler, now disciplining or exiling a recalcitrant prince.

Such relationships were an important element in forming Java Style: both European residents and Javanese *bupati* were linked in a complicity that expressed itself in terms of architecture and design. *Bupati* and residents both lived in mansions that combined neoclassical elements into a pattern that was essentially Javanese. Though they may have had different tastes and different attitudes, élite Javanese and Europeans, and indeed the wealthy Chinese, and Eurasians, lived in a common world.

The streamlined forms of art deco have become part of Java's everyday vernacular style: witness this roadside bench in Madura.

But this world was changing. Improvements in technology, communication and transportation had brought new wealth to Java's cities at the end of the 19th century. In the 20th century, private enterprise reached the countryside. A new Ethical Policy extended Dutch-language education beyond the European community, inevitably training a generation of Javanese that would demand change and equality. "Educate the Javanese!" wrote Raden Adjeng Kartini, a remarkable Dutch-educated noblewoman who has come to symbolize the power of those aspirations. Old worlds and new were in increasing tension during the first thirty years of the 20th century. Much of Java's *tempo doeloe* or 'good old days' version of a colonial life remained, but it was increasingly confronted with a more-quickly-paced industrialized future. Physically Java was changing. Roads and railroads crossed the island. There was a flowering of modernistic buildings made for new purposes: train stations, hotels for

The gateway marks the entrance to the alun-alun, *the sacred field north of the* kraton, *and the heart of the cities of Central Java.*

commercial travellers, factories and office blocks, hospitals and training schools.

Strangely enough, social distance between the Javanese and Europeans increased in these years: the colour bar dates to this period. Perhaps Europeans needed to separate themselves from their subjects, now that the Javanese were becoming educated, as reformist Islam brought many new confidence, and as nationalist activists made their presence felt. When the Great Depression hit in the 1930s the dream of a European Java was truly over. Java's economy, tuned to the production of export crops, was devastated. The countryside became terribly impoverished, the tension between nationalists and the Dutch government grew stronger. Java had still not recovered by the time the Japanese occupation of 1942 brought an end to the European domination of the island for good.

"Segala menyala-nyala, segala menyala-nyala." Everything is on fire. The words of Chairul Anwar, poet of Indonesia's national revolution, sum it up well enough. Four years of brutal occupation were succeeded by more suffering, as Java struggled against Dutch reimposition of colonial rule. The Republic of Indonesia was declared on 17 August 1945, but it took four years of armed struggle before the Dutch recognized the independent Republic of Indonesia.

The 1950s and 1960s alternated between the euphoria of independence and the continued struggle of nation building. Indonesia wrestled with awesome problems, including sharp regional conflicts and an almost totally decayed infrastructure. Inside Java there were deep political divisions that took an increasingly bitter toll. Soekarno, the nation's first President, could only walk the tightrope for so long. In 1965 an abortive Communist coup sparked a wave of violence that devastated the island.

In the wake of this trauma, a General Soeharto succeeded in consolidating power. By the 1970s, he was beginning to turn the economy around, rejecting a discredited economic nationalism and opening up to foreign investment. Soeharto's rule sparked nearly thirty years of rapid development and wealth-creation. Whilst concerns remain about the equity and sustainability of this growth, the last quarter of the 20th century saw Java once more moving forward.

Java today has a complex legacy. Visually it is a fascinating amalgam. The years of underdevelopment in the middle of the 20th century have preserved many of the buildings of the past, yet the breakneck development of the last twenty five years is transforming the landscape daily. Through it all, the independent Indonesians of Java remain oriented; their cultures are strong and encompassing, and owe little to the opinions and attitudes of foreign visitors.

Like a pilgrim circumambulating through the galleries of the Borobudur then, this book makes a procession around its centre. The Javanese make a virtue of indirection, so it would be too indelicate, too direct, (not to mention too difficult) to 'define' Java Style in analytical terms. Rather than go in for such a frontal attack, this book moves at a tangent to the target, looking inward and out, learning, and hopefully coming closer to the essence through those exertions. In keeping with the ancient classificatory schema that pervades Javanese symbolic thought, this book is divided into five parts: four plus one, the pivot and the four quarters. This introduction takes the broad view, followed by four chapters which each considers different themes or strains in Java Style: the great tradition, the *tempo doeloe,* modernisms and the contemporary. The great tradition refers to those styles created and crystallized in Java of the 14th century or so; the style of the colonial 19th century is second, called by some the *tempo doeloe* or the 'good old days'. Modernisms refers to those styles which spread around the world at the turn of the 20th century, and which still exert a hold on the Javanese idea of what is both tasteful and up-to-date, and the last chapter, contemporary homes, presents a selection of houses of recent design. Perhaps the future will give that style a name.

This is not a history book. Despite being titled after periods of time, each chapter includes a mix of the old and the contemporary. Each of the styles highlighted above is living and vital to Java Style, interpenetrating in complex ways. The most ancient court of Java is built to plans that resemble the 14th-century capital of Majapahit, in a series of pavilions and towers that owes nothing to later European ways of portraying power and authority. Yet the palace is outfitted with Victorian allegorical statuary, cast-iron columns, crystal chandeliers and art-nouveau stained glass.

In the remote teak-growing areas of East Java, villagers carve their large sleeping benches to resemble Raffles chairs, a design of the English Regency of 1815 or so. Java has perhaps the largest surviving inventory of 1920s art-deco buildings in the world: the armchairs on sale today in rural marketplaces replicate art-deco designs in softwood and rattan. In South Jakarta there is a neoclassical villa that is a fine example of the so-called Indo-European hybrid, a 19th-century building type created from neoclassical European detailing and masonry over the form of a traditional Java house. This building was removed from its original site and is now a restaurant. Every observer will have their own examples of the myriad ways Java juxtaposes and dislocates what seems at first glance like orderly history.

Ancient or made yesterday, buildings must serve the pressing needs of the world's most densely populated island, and its youthful, growing, and still under-developed society.

GLASS PAINTING

Reverse painting on glass was a popular folk art of the first forty years of the 20th century: it has recently enjoyed new popularity, with painters pursuing the medium as a fine art form, the most successful receiving major commissions. The paintings shown here however are from the older, less-refined folk tradition.

Religious subjects are popular in glass paintings, the second and third paintings in the top row here are representations of the Kaaba, in the holy mosque of Mecca. Possibly the single most popular image is a painting of a Javanese mosque, like the first one in the middle row at left. Most of these images include a modern car in the foreground as this one does. Scenes from the world of popular theatre are very common subjects, whether the stories are drawn from Hindu epics (third from left, middle row) or the rich stock of Muslim stories, like the striking painting first from left on the top row, which depicts the journey of Prince Marsuda to claim a holy talisman. Notice how much of the wayang style is incorporated into these characters, even though they represent devout Muslims. The clowns of the wayang are prized subjects of glass painting. They are often shown in modern settings, or socializing together (as in the second and fourth paintings in the lower row).

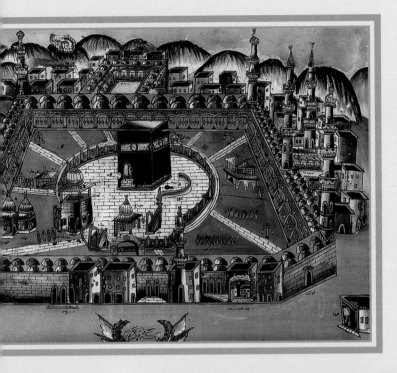

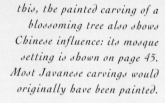

WOODCARVING

Java is heir to a rich legacy of different traditions of wood-carving. The low-relief carved door and brackets (above) in Pati on the North Coast are 19th-century copies of a Majapahit-style gateway. Wayang stylization is clear, as is the stylization of rock, cloud and plant motifs which was an important 15th-century innovation in Java.

Furniture, door- and archways, columns, dados, and screens, all could be carved and decorated. Sometimes outside influences can be clearly identified, as in the Chinese-influenced vase of plenty (second column from right), with its storks, plum blossoms and peonies. Left of

this, the painted carving of a blossoming tree also shows Chinese influence: its mosque setting is shown on page 43. Most Javanese carvings would originally have been painted.

The upper horizontal image, immediate right, shows a Kudus door, a high-relief open-work carving that is perhaps the most technically accomplished form on the island. Below it is a sample from a gilded 18th-century Batavia-style transom light.

The North-Coast town of Jepara retains a reputation as a centre of woodcarving and furniture making. The realistic scene on the facing page was created there.

the great

t r a d i t i o n

the great tradition

ARCHITECTURE AND ORNAMENT FROM JAVA'S TRADING AGE

Wood has long been the material of choice for domestic life in Java. Many fine woods grow here, but primary among them for building and furniture is teak, *Tectona grandis*. This noble wood, called *jati* in Javanese, a word denoting purity and truth, grows in great long trunks once highly prized for ships' masts. It was probably introduced to the region from India. Teakwood is hard and resistant to moisture and pests. It is cool to the skin, takes the blade well, and weathers to a smooth, slightly oily finish. Paired with palm and grass fibres, rattans and bamboo for texture, it provides strength and as much durability as can be expected in the humid tropics. Teak takes some eighty years to mature, and the plantations have suffered from neglect during WWII. Old pieces, their size speaking of the age of tree they came from, are now much prized by designers.

This love affair with wood may have prejudiced the Hindu-Buddhist Javanese against stone and brick construction in the early years of our era. When the Javanese did take to stone twelve hundred years ago the reliefs carved on stone temples show buildings predominantly made of wood. Despite the speed at which the Javanese learned and then mastered stone and also brick construction, wood was still the favourite for domestic architecture for many years to come.

The earliest standing stone buildings in Java are a series of small temples built around 750 CE in a dramatic, marshy plateau that forms the floor of a caldera complex on top of an active volcano. It is a weird setting, the Dieng Plateau, at 6,000 feet up, far from any centres of population, with its dreary mists, poisonous effusions and sulphur-coloured lakes. There can be little doubt that the Dieng Plateau was chosen as a building site for religious reasons. Its other-worldly atmosphere clearly marked it as an abode of the god-ancestors, Di Hyang, and the stone temples were constructed as a monument to them, not a convenience to man. The temples are small Hindu shrines, miniature cosmic mountains, following plans laid down in Indian religious texts, but with design motifs that for the most part have no clear correlate in India.

Once started, the Javanese took to stone and brick with a vengeance, over the course of the next few decades progressing from these small, delicate temples hardly large enough to shelter a priest performing ablutions on holy linga, to masterpieces like the Borobudur, which is the world's largest Buddhist monument, built without the aid of mortar between 770 and 800 CE. It is a veritable mountain of meditating Buddhas, stunning in the complex ways its architecture expresses the underlying Mahayana Buddhist philosophy of its architects. The Prambanan temples, consecrated in 856 CE, a time of Hindu revival on Java, have dramatic towers reaching skyward. The skillful juxtaposition of vertical shapes in horizontal ranks manipulates one's sense of perspective to emphasize the drama of the ensemble, echoed by the outline of Mt. Merapi rising in parabolic precision to the north.

The classic Austronesian wooden house—built on piles with curving and projecting roof ridges—is seen on the stone-carved reliefs at Borobudur and Prambanan, and later on reliefs on temples in East Java. It was apparently in common use from the 9th to 12th centuries at least. Houses raised on piles are practical in many ways, aiding ventilation in the tropical heat, keeping food, goods and people from dampness and moisture, and allowing houses to be built on river and wetland margins. But sometime around the 13th or 14th century, the preferred house in Central and East Java was one with floors on the ground, and the house on piles became less and less common, though they remained the dominant form in West Java.

This 14th-century lamp depicts a meditation pavilion, with its heavily carved columns and brick platform base.

The boundary between building and furniture is an open one in the Austronesian and classical Javanese pattern. If the basic building type is a four-posted roofed platform on legs, a small version of that makes for a bed or a couch. Leave out the roof and truncate the columns and you have a large platform for sitting and sleeping. Such a platform, known as *poade* on the Pasisir, made of wood and bamboo, remains the most popular item of furniture in Java today. Leave out the roof, and use woodcarving instead of a hanging textile as a backing between two columns, and you have a throne of a type very common on the old reliefs, *sesako,* a furniture type which survived until recently in South Sumatra as a mark of rank.

The additional furnishings of ancient Java were suited to these settings. Seats of European heights are rare in Indonesia's classical art, with the spectacular exception of the seated Buddha of Mendut. Even princes, kings and saints are depicted on the reliefs sitting on low platforms, some featuring elaborately

Temple reliefs from Borobudur (right) and Prambanan (below).

decorated backs. Boxes and parcels of various sizes are used for storage, often placed underneath the platforms or couches. Footed trays are a common element, suitable for making offerings of food and flowers. Incense burners and lamps of bronze or terracotta complete the setting. Hanging textiles demarkate space. Cylindrical bolsters are seen as supports for those seated on platforms. In the Borobudur reliefs, many of the figures wear a loose band around their waist. By leaning their knees against the belt, pulling it taught around the waist, they distribute weight more comfortably. Stools, some obviously made of cane, are also common.

It is an attractive organic tropical style. The predominant textures are of wood, bamboo, and palm fibres. Textiles and mats are everywhere, and the people depicted in the reliefs often wear wrapped textiles and go bare-chested. The wealthy among them make extravagant use of jewellery and hair ornaments. In the use of textiles, and in seating styles one can see clear continuities with later Java, though standards of dress have changed significantly. By the 14th century, the old living style reached an apogee of luxuriance in the capital of the Majapahit empire.

"Of all the buildings, none lack pillars, bearing fine carvings and coloured." The *Nagarakertagama* by Mpu Prapanca includes descriptions of the Majapahit capital. His text confirms the archeological evidence, that Majapahit houses were built on brick platforms, some with river-pebble flooring. Within the walled compounds, "there were elegant pavilions roofed with aren fibre, like the scene in a painting... The petals of the *katangga* were sprinkled over the roofs, for they had fallen in the wind. The roofs were like maidens with flowers arranged in their hair, delighting those who saw them." *Aren* is the black fibre of the sugar palm, still used for roofs in important Balinese buildings.

While brick was used in Java throughout the classical era, the architects of 14th- and 15th-century Majapahit truly mastered it. Making use of a mortar of vine sap and palm sugar, Majapahit temples have a strong geometrical quality. They instill an imposing feeling of verticality, a sense which is achieved with a series of many small horizontal lines. Many of the remains visible today give an almost art-deco sense of streamlining and proportion. At any rate, they are elegant expressions of the qualities of their material.

Brick was also used for long walls, ramparts and gateways enclosing large compounds in a sprawling capital city shot through with canals and brick-lined reservoirs. Water was everywhere in ancient Majapahit, running through the city in terracotta plumbing, from bathing places and water temples to house and palace compounds, and in the canals that linked to the sea.

Also at this time there is the first evidence for houses with load-bearing walls. A relief at Candi Tegawangi shows this clearly, as do a great number of small model terracotta houses excavated in Trowulan. Why this change? That stone and brick were no longer considered the sole province of temples, but were used extensively for domestic architecture, may have something to say about changing religious beliefs or the growth of a merchant class outside of the confines of court. Evidence for resident foreign communities has

led some to suggest that masonry houses were introduced to follow Chinese, Indian, or perhaps Vietnamese, models.

Majapahit's flowering did not last. By the second half of the 15th century the thriving trading sultanates of Java's North Coast had eclipsed her power. But the style and way of life of the Majapahit capital was to live on for many years as a kind of ideal, in places like Cirebon on the north coast. Bali in particular was heavily influenced by Majapahit, or at least by the ideal of Majapahit, and in many ways the Balinese believe themselves to be the true heirs of the Kingdom of the Bael Tree.

Lifestyles changed in Java in the one hundred and fifty years that followed Majapahit's decline. For one thing, Java was now extremely well linked to a greater Southeast-Asian region, and events occurred on a regional scale, with no single power able to dominate as Majapahit had. Java was closely allied to the great port of Malacca on the Straits further north, supplying it with nearly all of its rice needs, sent in huge transport junks that dwarfed the first Portuguese carracks to encounter them. Chinese presence in the region was vigorous, with the Ming Dynasty in a moment of rare openness to the world. And a particularly mystical sort of Islam was expanding through the island, stimulating creativity in literature, art and architecture. This was the age of the *wali sanga*, the Nine Saints of Islam, whose adventures and exploits are popular stories in Java yet.

It was during these years that the first of the great Southeast-Asian mosques was built, in Demak according to tradition. The main feature of these mosques is a double-, triple- or even quintuple-peaked roof, on a square plan, the topmost roof supported by the four large master pillars, the

Medallion in stone from the Mantingan mosque on the North Coast. The endless knot pattern is characteristically syncretic.

soko guru. Walls and towers of some of these mosques are built in brickwork that resembles the brick temples of Majapahit: Kudus and Cirebon are most striking in this respect. Another interesting feature of many of these mosques, and the palaces that were built at the same time, is that they make use of medallions of ceramics inset into the brick. The mosques of Kudus and Demak feature Vietnamese ceramics which were clearly designed and made for that precise purpose. In the years that followed, mosques on this pattern were built across the *nusantara,* from North Sumatra eastward to Mindanao in the southern Philippine islands, wherever Islam established itself in the archipelago.

Cirebon, especially, still yields evidence of how the great merchant princes of the Pasisir must have lived: the present Kraton Kasepuhan is an early 17th-century continuation of an older palace compound. As in Majapahit, the basic form is of a series of pavilions surrounded by a brick wall, the wall now studded with ceramic plates or tiles. The carpentry in these pavilions is increasingly complex, featuring roof beams which radiate out from a central point, in a pattern different from the the rectangular frames which seem to predate them. Complex carved brackets appear to be new introductions from this period. Woodcarving and other arts become more abstract, more geometricized. Old motifs such as the lotus are reused in the service of Islam, and Chinese rock and cloud shapes make their appearance here as well. The later Kraton Kanoman makes use of European-inspired innovations: arches and masonry columns for the *pendopo.*

Pendopos sheltered the functioning of Javanese states, with specific ones allotted to the law courts, the clergy and the king and his ministers for their public appearances. The symbolic importance of the buildings to the legitimacy of the rulers was carried to new lengths in the late 18th century, when the court of

Pakubuwono II of Mataram at Kartasura was transferred to a new capital near the village of Solo. Leading the grand procession of all the court officials were the two *Waringin,* or Banyan trees, Dewadaru and Jayadaru, wrapped in silk and carried by officials especially appointed for the job. The descendants of these

The block-style stone gateway of this mosque preserves the geometric shapes of the architectural styles of ancient East Java.

trees still stand in the square to the north of the court. Then the *pendopo* known as the *bangsal pangrawit* 'in its whole' was lifted and carried to the new site by the *kalang* and *gowong* officials. Following were the elephants of the king, with their keepers and other officials, et cetera, etc. By the time the king had arrived, the *pendopo* had been set in its new place, and the regalia and royal entourage were quickly moved to their proper positions around it. The king gave his audience, declaring that henceforth Solo, now to be called Surakarta, was to be his capital.

Today, the courts of Java preserve the ancient forms, though the trim is often modern. In the layouts of the Kraton Kasepuhan in Cirebon, and in the more recent Kratons of Solo and Yogyakarta, some scholars

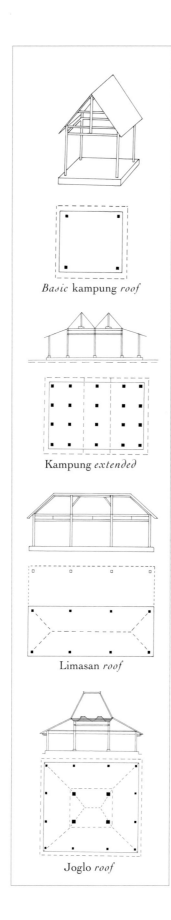

Basic kampung *roof*

Kampung *extended*

Limasan *roof*

Joglo *roof*

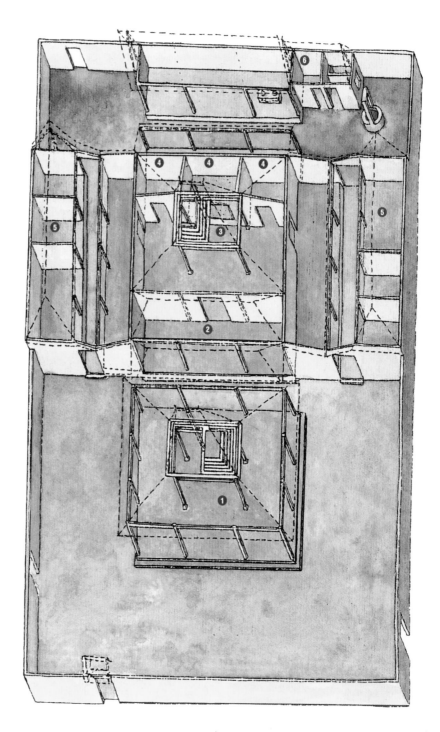

The layout of a Javanese house. The pendopo ❶ can clearly be seen in front, the dotted lines indicating the joglo roof form, and the tumpang sari *ceiling structure seen from above. Beyond is the* peringgitan *or* veranda ❷ , *and the* dalem ❸, which also has a joglo *roof, with* tumpang sari. *At the rear of the* dalem *are the three* senthong ❹. *On either side of the main structures are the* gandok *or outbuildings* ❺ , *with the kitchen, well and toilet at the rear of the house compound* ❻.

see echoes of Majapahit. Ceremonials are still important to the *kratons,* and there is a busy life of courtiers,
and court-supported arts. Although they may not
have any official roles in the running of the state
today, the palaces are still places of prestige, still able
to arbitrate Java Style.

*Market-day life
goes on outside a
walled Javanese
house compound.
The forms of
the* joglo *roof
can be seen behind
the walls.*

Traditional Javanese houses, like Balinese ones, are
usually built in a walled compound. The wealthier make their walls of masonry, other walls are of split
bamboo or timber. Living walls of interlinked trees or
vines are common in rural areas. Orientation is never
ignored: in Central Java houses face south towards the
sea wherever possible, and they are laid out on a
north-south axis.

The Javanese look at houses and see roofs. Houses
are classified according to their roof forms, and houses are organized by the placement of the columns
which support roofs. Walls, it bears repeating, are
secondary: their placement is determined by the roof-
carrying columns. In the simplest Javanese house, four
columns of equal height are braced by a double layer
of trusses. From the centre of two of the trusses rise
two columns, which in turn support a roof beam.

This *kampung* roof falls away in two directions on
either side of the beam. Of course, this simple shape
may often be extended, added to and combined with
other roof shapes.

The most common roof type in Javanese houses is
the *limasan,* created by extending the *kampung* model
to a rectangular plan, with additional pairs of columns
at either end. The basic shape is created by the fact
that the roof beam does not run the full length of the
rectangular building, rather it extends over the innermost set of columns. This means the *limasan* roof has
four slopes, two along the longer and two along the
shorter axes. The typical *limasan* has four slopes and
five ridges, and it begins to give an emphasis to the
central area between the innermost four columns.

The most characteristic Javanese roof form for
houses, and the most complex, is the *joglo.* The portion of the roof that sites over the innermost four
columns is much steeper, almost a pyramid, except
that it comes to two points rather than a single one.
The *joglo* does not use king posts as does the
limasan or *kampung* roof. Rather, the master pillars
are sometimes taller than the outer ones. And resting
on top of the central four pillars are layers of wooden
blocks, which step back into the centre, and out to
the sides. The outermost blocks support the roof that
rises steeply above, the inner layers form a stepped
pyramidal ceiling. The timbers of the inner layers are
often heavily worked, carved and gilded. This ceiling
of stepped timbers, the *tumpang sari,* is usually the
most intensely decorated area of the traditional
Javanese house.

The *pendopo,* mentioned earlier, features in many
wealthier homes. If there is no permanent *pendopo,* a
temporary one can be erected for special occasions.
Also in some crowded urban areas, masonry walls
might be erected around the *pendopo.*

The house proper is the *omah,* a word with an Austronesian root, expressed in the Malay *rumah,* etc. It is usually square in plan, with either a *joglo* or *limasan* roof. Sometimes, between the *omah* and the *pendopo,* a special transitional area is defined. This is the *peringgitan,* the space for the *ringgit,* meaning *wayang* or puppet play. When a *wayang* is commissioned for a home, it is performed here. The *omah* is organized as a progression from front to back. First is the *emperan,* a semi-veranda, often enclosed with moveable wooden panels. Inside this space, visitors are received. There is often a large bench on the right side of the space, for sitting, or the place where the young man of the house will sleep. The traditional Javanese doors that have appeared on the antiques market, are from either the outer wall of the *emperan,* or the walls between the *emperan* and the rest of the *dalem.* It is the interior wall that is most heavily decorated.

Moving inside the *dalem* involves crossing another threshold. Here a high door jamb often emphasizes the sensitive nature of the transition. In a *joglo* house the columns of the central section of the roof rise in a dark room usually lit only from the doorway. If the house is a large one, and has extensions built to the west and east, the centre of the house is often rather empty, its use reserved for ceremonial occasions. If the house does not have large extensions, the centre of the *dalem* will be the actual as well as spiritual focus of house life. Furthest to the back are the three small enclosed rooms or *senthong,* kept quite distinct from the rest of the house. The outer two rooms are traditionally used for storing rice and agricultural tools, or

perhaps for meditation and aesthetic practice. The central room is the most highly charged: this is the realm of the rice goddess, Sri, in south Central Java often conflated with Nyai Loro Kidul, the goddess of the Southern Sea.

The *senthong tengah* is typically very small, with a raised floor, often curtained off from the house proper. In many cases it resembles more an enclosed bed than a room *per se.* It is here that incense is burnt for ceremonies, and in some areas the first rice grains of the harvest are placed here. In wealthy village houses in Central Java it is flanked by a pair of mirrors and a pair of cabinets for holding important textiles, emphasizing the importance of symmetry in the arrangements of this part of the house. On the floor in front of the *senthong* is the *loro blonyo,* the inseparable pair of statues, male and female, in bridal attire, representing Dewi Sri and her male companion Raden Sadono. Paired spittoons, textiles, in Madura wooden geese, complete the setup in front of the *senthong tengah.*

Outside of the *omah* are typically a number of outbuildings. In a large compound these buildings are more important for daily life than the *omah* itself. The well is typically placed on the eastern side, as are the areas for food preparation.

The modern houses of Java's cities typically lack all this paraphernalia of tradition. Even if, at first glance, houses owe little to the old patterns, it is remarkable how often echoes of the Central Javanese house can be felt in new structures, especially where space allows an unconstrained organization of elements.

In the 16th and 17th centuries, a new force had arrived on the Javanese scene. The arrival of the Europeans was to herald many developments for Java, not least the eventual adoption of brick and masonry house construction in Java's cities. It is perhaps fitting then that the story of European power in Java can be said to begin with a single building.

In 1610 the Dutch were attempting to create a base in Jayakarta, a small port once courted by the Portuguese, but now controlled by the powerful pepper trading Sultanate of Bantam. The prince of Jayakarta was restless under Bantam's rule, and susceptible to Dutch ministrations. In 1615 he made what was to be a fatal mistake: he granted permission to the aggressive young Dutch factor, Jan Pieterszoon Coen, to build a two-storey warehouse in coral stone.

This single building proved the key to Holland's eventual conquest of Java. Sultan Agung, ruling from Kota Gede in Central Java saw it only too well: "Jacatra hath a thorne in her foote, which [I] must take the pains to pluck out, for fear the whole body should be endangered. This thorn is the castle of the Hollanders, who have now so fortified themselves [through bribery] that they regard not the king nor his country, but set him at defiance." And defy the king they did. By 1619, after withstanding a siege of their warehouse-fort (an attack marked more by the disunity of the besiegers than the heroism of the besieged), the Dutch sacked the native town, and established their dominance over the city they renamed 'Batavia'.

Buildings in stone and masonry were as much about power as they were about shelter. With the example of Batavia on their minds, Java's local rulers discouraged masonry buildings when and where they could, guarding the privilege for their own palaces and mosques. Batavia of the 17th and 18th centuries was a brick-and-masonry city surrounded by fortifications. Laced with canals, fronted by masonry row houses with shared side walls, it actually owed more to Southern Chinese models than to Dutch ones. We know the Dutch imported bricks from Holland, perhaps as ship's ballast, or when local supplies were inadequate. The Chinese—crucial to the economic life of the new city—built in brick whenever possible.

Old Batavia was very much of an anomaly in Java, in terms of its buildings and city plan. Initially, as an expression of a European power under constant threat, Batavia yielded little to the dictates of local climate and culture. The results of this stubbornness were to prove disastrous, as Batavia's residents paid the price in discomfort and disease. By the end of the 18th century, Batavia had become famous as a deathtrap of fevers

The upper storey of the Fatahillah Museum. Once the seat of colonial power in Batavia, the building preserves a generous scale, with massive timber beams and floorboards.

and fluxes. In the eyes of an English observer, "Never were national prejudices and national taste so injudiciously misapplied, as in the attempt to assimilate those of Holland to the climate and soil of Batavia." By the end of the 18th century, deforestation in the foothills had caused silting in the canals. This further degraded the already-difficult environment of Batavia. Europeans in Java would need new designs, new houses and new lifestyles if they were to survive, and if they were to have any impact on lifestyles of the Javanese.

Islam made its way to Java through the trading ports of the North Coast. The famous mosque of Demak, above, is reckoned to be Java's oldest. In its walls are found Vietnamese ceramics which must have been specially commissioned: the shapes are derived from the conventions of Javanese woodcarving and brickwork. The use of ceramic rather than stone is likely to have been in imitation of the mosques of Persia. The mosque at Mantingan, left, is new, the stone medallions in its walls are roughly contemporary with Demak. They represent a specifically Javanese Islamic sensibility, Islamic in their abstraction, yet at times representing older Javanese themes like the meditation pavilion surrounded by forest.

The Menara Kudus Mosque—one of the island's older mosques—is a popular pilgrimage point, preserving the tomb of one of the nine Islamic saints of Java. Its brickwork is reminiscent of the Hindu-Buddhist period, its three-tiered pyramidal roof is a classic of the great Southeast-Asian mosque design of the 15th century onwards. The brick minaret, shaped like the kul-kul towers of Balinese Hindu temples, shelters a large skinned drum and a wooden slit drum. The peaked roof is a 1920s renovation with terracotta tiles replacing wooden ones, and glass windows inserted between the roof tiers. The ensemble is topped with a mastaka or crown roof ornament.

◆

Arguably the most atmospheric of the shrines of the saints of Islam is the Mesjïd Sunan Giri, near Gresik, some thirty miles from Surabaya. Its woodcarving seems to date back five hundred years; it is remarkably well preserved, retaining the original gold and red lacquer colour scheme. The pavilion shelters the tomb of the Sunan Giri, and is considered a spiritually potent place.

The Kraton Kanoman
was founded in 1677 by
Sultan Anom I, as one of
two main kraton or
palaces in the North-
Coast city of Cirebon.
In the outer area of the
kraton, or siti inggil, are
masonry versions of the
classic pendopo form.
As in Demak, ceramics
are embedded into the
plastered walls. The
squat split-gates with
their pyramidal peaks
are something of a
Cirebon emblem.

The early-17th-century siti inggil *compound of the Kasepuhan Palace of Cirebon preserves the legacy of Majapahit, with its small* pendopo *on soft carved brick bases. Particularly striking here is the woodcarving of the* pendopo *columns, 1940s copies preserving the form of the ancient originals. An innovation here is the use of brackets branching out from the main column. The Semar Tinandu pavilion (below) has two triple-bracketed columns.*

The Sunan Gunung Jati, or Lord of the Teak Mountain, was one of the most senior of the of Nine Saints of Islam in Java. His 400-year-old tomb on the foothills of Mt. Ciremai outside Cirebon is one of Java's most important pilgrimage points. When pieces of porcelain covering the enclosure break they are replaced with new pieces brought by well-wishers. Today the porcelains are mostly of European or Japanese origin.

The tombs of the nine saints of Javanese Islam, the wali sanga, are highly auspicious places for prayer and meditation. At left, one young man recites Koranic verses at the tomb of Sunan Giri. The atmosphere of such holy places in Java is an intensely charged one; so complete is the atmosphere that it can unite disparate visual elements: the weathered wooden tiles and roof ornaments, the blank undecorated wooden walls of the tomb enclosures and modern ceramic tiles seem to fit easily into the ensemble.

◆

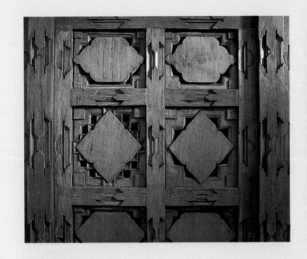

Trusmi outside Cirebon, on the North Coast of West Java, is a traditional centre of some of the most excellent batik-making in Java. The mosque preserves Javanese woodcarving forms in conjunction with brickwork gateways and walls. The carved column brackets which support the gateway roof were introduced to Java only at the tail end of the Majapahit period. The closely packed roofscape is characteristic of the pattern of the typical Javanese house compound.

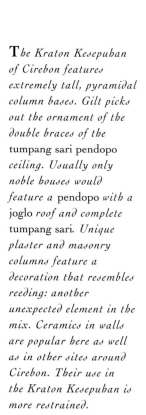

The Kraton Kesepuhan
of Cirebon features
extremely tall, pyramidal
column bases. Gilt picks
out the ornament of the
double braces of the
tumpang sari pendopo
ceiling. Usually only
noble houses would
feature a pendopo with a
joglo roof and complete
tumpang sari. Unique
plaster and masonry
columns feature a
decoration that resembles
reeding: another
unexpected element in the
mix. Ceramics in walls
are popular here as well
as in other sites around
Cirebon. Their use in
the Kraton Kesepuhan is
more restrained.

The tumpang sari
ornamentation in this
Solo Kraton pendopo is
complemented by the full
drama of a European
crystal chandelier.
Ornamentation of this
detail and luxury could
only be appropriate for
the highest houses of the
land, anyone else would
be committing a kind of
presumption that would
be anathema to Javanese
sensibilities. The gilt
figurines at top left are
part of the regalia of the
Sultan, carried by court
retainers during
processions and placed
around the throne
during full audiences.
Such practices are
common to the kings of
Southeast Asia.

◆

Prayer leaders and those most directly involved in feasts of blessing are seated on the floor of pavilions of the Kraton of Sumenep at Madura. Other guests will use the formal European chairs outside the main hall. The remarkable chair, left, features the naga or water dragon. Carving on Madurese grave screens, far left, is suffused with energy, movement and organic luxuriance. In a visual treat, the faces of guardian spirits and water beasts emerge from dense foliage.

Kota Gede south of Yogyakarta was one of the old capitals of Mataram. At the turn of the century, many of its wealthier residents built houses combining traditional Javanese elements and the materials and motifs of the early 20th century. The emperan or semi-veranda above is restrained; the house left features cool, polished concrete tiles, carved column capitals and brackets.

◆

A *Central Javanese house in Solo preserves the classic forms, with some variation. A masonry wall—albeit one pierced with windows and wide doorways—partially encloses the tiled* pendopo. *Rather than being ornately carved, the timbers of the* tumpang sari *are painted in contrasting colours—an art-deco touch. The central* senthong, *below, is curtained off, but the carvings leave no doubt that this is the ritual centre of the building.*

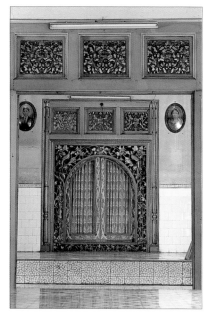

The dalem of this classic Central Javanese house, also in Solo, gives a sense of the dark, closed-in atmosphere thought suitable for most such spaces. The paired mirrors and consoles on either side of the senthong tengah are a common feature of finer old Javanese homes. The carving and etched glass in the doors to the two lesser senthong, below, are ornate in a manner that recalls both Chinese and European influences.

Traditional houses of East Java and Pasisir feature carved and painted doors or wall panels, in distinct regional styles. Most famous of all are the doors from Kudus, near Mt. Muria. The carving is detailed and in relatively high relief, and window panels are carved clear through, forming screens. Antique Kudus doors have become prized items, and they are now transplanted to modern homes and hotels — like this one in Malang, East Java.

The well is traditionally the first part of a Javanese house compound to be built, once ritual procedure has ensured that a selected site is clear of malevolent presences. In houses and palaces, water gardens are a common theme, and the Javanese appreciate too the beauty and spiritual significance of the water lily and the lotus flower, like those at left, from a Yogyakarta house compound.

The charm of Javanese towns of the North Coast lies in the eclectic combination of elements. At left, brick gateways in a Majapahit pattern front a house with art-nouveau-inspired carved doors, columns and column brackets. Terracotta roof ridge tiles decorated with bits of broken porcelain are an unmistakable mark of the Pasisir. Ornamental arches and gateways are common in Java — marking boundaries being a preoccupation of local officials.

tempo

d o e l o e

tempo doeloe

THE EUROPEAN NEOCLASSICAL IN JAVA

"They fought very valiantly for their ancestral customs [the Batavians of earlier times], but very few returned to tell of the fight. Since then, people have reflected that a live Netherlands-Indian is better than a dead Hollander. And giving up a fight, in which defeat was all but certain, and success worse than useless, they have all effected a compromise with the climate."

Notable for its representation of a Raffles chair, this print of a Madurese prince was published around 1856 as part of the Netherlands East Indies Types *series by C. W. Meiling.*

Dutch observer Augusta de Wit, writing in 1912 sums up the design sensibility of the 19th and early 20th centuries in Java, a period when European power in the island was at its peak. For want of a better term, this volume dubs that sensibility *tempo doeloe*. The words, the Dutch-style spelling for the Malay words (*tempo* coming by way of Portuguese) for the 'time before' or 'the good old days' call up a rich set of associations of a style and way of life that was adapted to

the tropical climate, and which was unique to Java and the Netherlands Indies.

Loose *batik* clothing worn at home, *sarongs* and long, lacy *kebaya* blouses, evening promenades along wide tree-lined boulevards, the endless plates of the spicy *rijstaffel* served by a veritable army of servants at the club: these were the elements of the *tempo-doeloe* life for the privileged of the colony of Java. One element of the colonial house summarized this style above all: the veranda, with its potted palms, its classical columns, cool concrete or marble floors, often covered with split bamboo matting, and deep overhanging roofs in terracotta tile. Here Java's élite lived a life of leisure, arrayed on fine wooden furniture in Regency and Empire styles, always working hard at keeping cool.

The irony is rich: this 'compromise with the climate' was no retreat. For the Europeans, it was their deep-seated confidence in their right to rule that allowed them to adapt, to let go of Amsterdam ways and try new ones. *Tempo-doeloe* style was a victory and an expression of the rightness and inevitability of the imperial enterprise of the Netherlands Indies. As such, it will always be associated with the doomed dream of 'Europe-in-Java', and the terrible human cost of colonialism. But to the extent that it is possible to think about design without thinking of the society which created it, *tempo-doeloe* style must be seen as rich, and creative. It was undeniably unique.

This uniqueness is worth exploring. Though architecture and furniture designs from Europe were important inputs, *tempo-doeloe* style for houses was a local creation. The architects of Java's classical era built temples that followed the classical texts but resembled nothing in India. The builders of colonial style followed handbooks from Europe. The classical orders as set out in translations of Palladio's *Five*

Published in a four-volume series in 1881 from older drawings by J.C. Rappard this chromolithograph depicts a domestic moment. The veranda here is protected from rain by large painted bamboo chick blinds, anchored to the veranda rail.

Books of Architecture can be seen reproduced all over the island. But in most cases they form elements in buildings that in overall conception and layout owe little to Europe, and much to Java.

Tempo-doeloe style was an élite style to be sure, but it was not the exclusive preserve of Europeans. It was a common ground between Europeans locally- and foreign-born, and wealthy or privileged Chinese and Javanese. The Javanese élite—who clung to much of their privilege and ceremony, but held little of their former power—helped to forge this style too, and drew from it for their own purposes.

In the beginning, the princes of Java designed sitting rooms with European-style furniture in order to please their European guests; soon this exotica became more widespread. In 1816 Raffles wrote that "in the European provinces, many of the rooms of the chiefs are furnished with looking glasses, chairs, tables, etc. Most of these were introduced for the accommodation of European visitors, but are now gradually becoming luxuries, in which the chiefs take delight." Fifty years later, this process had reached the point where the Javanese élite were fully conversant with European styles and forms of furniture, and sure of their tastes in these matters.

As the Dutch moved to the southern outskirts of Batavia they began to build houses on more generous and open scale. After the defeat of Javanese leader Diponegoro in 1830, the sense of security was complete, and the walls and fortifications around Dutch settlements came down. The new kind of home built over the next eighty years has been termed an 'Indo-European hybrid'.

Louis Couperus, the great Dutch writer of the *fin de siècle*, described such a house in his highly atmospheric novel *The Hidden Force:* "the residency lay far back in its garden. Low and vivid in the darkness of the *waringin* trees, it lifted the zigzag outline of its tiled roofs, one behind the other, into the shadow of the garden behind it, with a primitive line that seemed to date it: a roof over each room, receding into one long outline of irregular roofs. In front however, the white pillars of the front veranda rose, with the white pillars of the portico, tall bright and stately, with wide intervals, with a large, welcoming spaciousness, with an expansive and imposing entrance, as if to a palace. Through the open doors, the central gallery was seen in dim perspective, running through to the back and lit by a single, flickering light."

The description captures the architectural essence of the Indo-European house, as well as its desire to impress. (His model was the sugar town of Pasuruan in East Java). A classically proportioned veranda complete with Tuscan or Doric order columns runs the entire width of the house, opening by a series of large doors, or doors and windows, to a first inner room on the same proportions. Beyond this room a central gallery runs lengthwise through to the back of the house, with rooms arranged symmetrically on either side, opening finally on a back room that matches the first, taking the entire width of the house. Typically a smaller veranda at the back gave out onto the back garden and its outbuildings: pavilions, the kitchen, buildings for servants, other buildings for specific functions: stables, storehouses, bathhouses and the like.

The roofs over each room are in the Javanese *limasan* pattern, a long lengthways ridge and four panels falling at equal angles to each side. The roofs form a series of ridges, one over each room or set of rooms. In this respect, and in the organization of space from the front moving progressively to the back, the hybrid house follows the Javanese model exactly. Architectural historian Yulianto Soemaljo identifies the veranda with the *pringgitan* of the traditional Javanese house, the front room with the *dalem,* and the back rooms and last gallery with the *senthong.*

"For to be cool or not to be cool, that is the great question," asserted Madame De Wit, and the veranda or *voorgalerij,* was the coolest place in the house. "For the sake of coolness one has marble floors or Javanese matting instead of carpets, cane-bottomed chairs and settees in lieu of velvet-covered furniture,

This original of this print by A Van Pers was published in Batavia in 1851. It depicts Huishoudsters (Nyai), *or local women who were common law wives of Dutch men.*

gauze hangings for draperies of silks and brocade. For in this climate to sit in a velvet chair is to realize the sensations of Saint Laurence, without the sustaining consciousness of martyrdom."

Coolness was not the only aspect of the veranda. Harriet Ponder, an English writer drawn to Java observed that this space "is the pride, the shop window, as it were, of every house, large and small, for, having no front wall, except perhaps a stone railing and pillars, it is in full view from the road." Nineteenth-century photographs of proud families are invariably taken on the veranda. The inner rooms were for formal functions with "chairs lined up against the wall as though in readiness for an eternal reception" (Couperus), but the veranda was where daily life happened. Here is where the ladies of the house encountered Java, in the form of Chinese cloth merchants, other traders or petty officials come on official business.

Making a virtue of a necessity: mosquito nets are sometimes still needed in Java. This example is of a hundred-year-old fine lace. The special silver hook and tape are used to hold the netting open during the daytime.

European neoclassical trends in design stand out for the way that they have been embraced and enveloped by the myriad streams of Javanese interior and architectural design. Neoclassical styles of the turn of the 19th century are still a dominant element in contemporary furniture and interiors, in the cities, towns and remarkably, in the villages of Java. Of course the neoclassical furniture of this period was a real high-water mark for Europe, with designs being revived again and again into the early 20th century. Still, the impact of a relatively limited set of designs in Java was remarkably deep, even deeper than the impact of the neoclassical in America. The proof is in the way many of the designs can today be found in rustic forms in the villages of Java, as benches or large chairs executed in heavy teak. The charm of this 'rustification' of English models is key to the current popularity of Javanese country furniture in Europe and the United States.

So what explains the vigour of this influence in Java? For one thing, the emergence of the neoclassical styles coincided with times of rapid development and change in Java, changes exemplified in the rule of Daendels and the Raffles interregnum. What furniture that was imported to Java (and there was likely to have been very little) would have been of English or French manufacture, and these were the centres of the neoclassical revival. The English had recently begun the large-scale manufacture of furniture in European styles in India, and it is possible that either some of this furniture made its way to Java, at least during the interregnum, or that entrepreneurs saw opportunities to copy such efforts, and offer new designs.

Of great importance was the suitability of neoclassical designs to tropical climates. They looked equally good with or without upholstery, and designs that worked without upholstery were certainly more suited to tropical heat. Neoclassical furniture could use cane seats and backs as well, the ultimate in coolness and comfort. Ebony chairs with seats of woven tropical rattan had reached Europe from Batavia in the 1650s, and caning had subsequently become extremely popular in Europe, though the vogue petered out eventually.

The two factors then—historical circumstance and

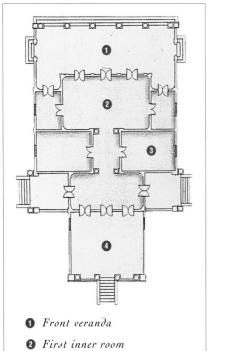

1 *Front veranda*

2 *First inner room*

3 *Bedrooms, opening on the
central gallery*

4 *Back veranda*

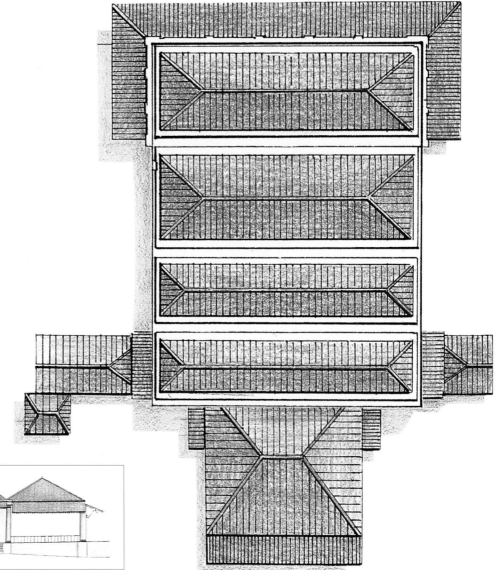

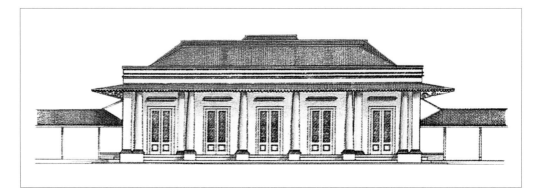

The Batavia residence of the
governor of West Java, extended
in the 1960s to suit its new
duties as Jakarta's City Hall.
The front elevation (right)
shows its classical proportions,
with Tuscan order columns. The
plan and side elevation show the
progression of limasan roof
ridges moving towards the back
of the house, as seen in many
traditional Javanese houses.

suitability to climate—explain the depth of the impact of the neoclassical in Java. The question of whether there is some deeper resonance between Java Style and neoclassical forms and proportions is perhaps already moot: by now, the neoclassical is a deep strain in a long-lasting Java Style.

There is one item of furniture that sums up the impact of the neoclassical more than any other: the Raffles chair. Its name is explained by the idea that its use was popularized during Raffles' brief rule as Lieutenant-Governor over Java, from 1811 to 1816. So prevalent is the Raffles chair, in surviving images and in photographs of the second half of the 19th century, (and in today's homes) that there can be little doubt that it was manufactured in Java from an early date.

The inventory of 1779 for the estate of the Madurese Prince Panembahan Tjakraningrat mentions there being 24 "Jepara chairs", for the front gallery. As "high-backed chairs" and "round men's chairs" are described elsewhere, the conclusion is that these chairs were clearly recognizable as being made in Jepara, a Pasisir town that had long been known for the quality of its woodcarving.

The basic design of the Raffles chair is usually credited to the brilliant English designer Thomas Sheraton who published his most influential designs between 1794 and 1803. A chair which has a similar profile to the Raffles chair does appear on plate 33 of Sheraton's *Drawing Book* of 1794. The basic shape is of thin arms arching down, forming a scroll that sits above a vase-shaped dowel. The line continues down to the straight, tapering reeded front legs. The shapes are heavily ornamented, but Sheraton wrote "the mere outlines of any of them will serve as patterns either for painted or mahogany chairs, by leaving out the ornaments for the mahogany".

A stylish image of colonial leisure from 1908. Our subject wears a cool cotton jacket over loose batik pants, the ideal outfit for lounging in the rear veranda of the house. Much veranda furniture was made of rattan like this.

But there are striking differences between Sheraton's chairs and the Raffles chairs so common in Java. Sheraton's designs have thin and elegant top rails, with vertically oriented decoration joining a low horizontal stretcher. The Raffles chairs typically have a strong horizontal back rail, with horizontally oriented crossbars usually quite high above the back of the seat. Most importantly, the broad rail usually projects beyond the sides of the seat, and takes a concave form to welcome the sitter's back. Importantly too, the rear legs are swept sharply backwards.

It is clear that the Raffles chair is a later development: its curving, extended back and swept back legs reflecting the explicit influence of designs revived from ancient Greece. Outside of Java, the models most similar are American designs of 1815 and the heavier English-Regency work of 1810 to 1820. Did Raffles popularize the Raffles Chair in Java? If folk memory gets it right, it means that the style was current in Java at the very moment we first see it in Europe and America. Could this design be original to Java? It does not matter: through longevity, through use, Java has claimed it now.

Palms and terracotta floor tiles define the cool (if slightly damp) veranda of the Teater Kecil, a drama collective based in an old bungalow in Jakarta. A marble-top table accompanied by Empire-inspired rattan-seated chairs and terracotta pedestals complete the formula.

Java's climate allows for a perfusion of greenery. Epiphytes are plants which root on the surface of other plants, especially trees. Because they require little soil and are rather hardy they make excellent garden plants in Java. Birds' nests predominate in this small garden, hanging from the veranda and in the tree at centre. Java's gardens make great use of pots and planters: here can be seen a classically inspired planter in front, and a large Chinese dragon jar beyond the bench.

The Protestant Church at Semarang was consecrated in 1794. At the time it was among the grandest (and most beautiful) colonial buildings in Java. Today's interior is the result of an 1895 restoration; practically no changes have been made since then. The church is built on an octagonal plan, the nave encircled by eight large Corinthian columns, with four entry porches of Greek inspiration.

The church is a hybrid of neoclassical and Renaissance styles. The 1895 restoration by the Dutch architects H.P.A. de Werde and W. Westmaas preserves the typical adaptations of the European neoclassical to the tropics: rattan seating on hardwood chairs, and cool floor tiles.

This classic pavilion is the Bangsal Trajumas, one of a pair of pavilions in the Srimanganti Courtyard of the Kraton Yogyakarta. The Bangsal Trajumas and its counterpart were used for important ceremony-laden public functions, in this case, as a law court. As seen here and in the images on right, the architectural detailing of the Kraton Yogya — stained glass, statuettes and chandeliers — adds a Victorian feeling onto the old Javanese forms. The Kraton is built on a human scale, neither imposing nor forbidding, except to those who perceive the ritual power that is traditionally said to reside in the palace.

◆

In the two hundred years since the courts of Java came into an intimate relationship with the Dutch government, they had time to evolve a style that harmonized traditional ideas with what the Javanese thought the best in European ornament. The impact of European ideas of military splendour led to the adoption of gold braid and the double-breasted coat, as worn by the Solo palace guard above. The portrait of the Sunan of Solo shows the adoption of the red velvet coat into royal costume: the gilt frame is a fine example of a bending of Javanese ornamentation to a European-derived purpose.

◆

The Pendopo Agung of the Mangkunegaran, left, was originally built in 1810, but rebuilt earlier this century to a much more dramatic height, by Dutch architect Thomas Karsten, working in close collaboration with Prince Mangkunegaran VII. Being the largest pendopo on the island, it is still the site of public ceremonies of the palace. The building many now think of as being one of the classic Javanese spaces was designed by a Dutch architect: Java Style is full of such contradiction.

Mangkunegaran pavilion, above — designed by Thomas Karsten working in collaboration with Prince Mangkunegoro VII between 1917 and 1920. Its main innovations are its octagonal plan, and the use of a number of enjoyable variations on traditional Javanese double-truss beamwork. But most importantly it was designed for a kind of use which was new to its era: receptions in a Europeanized style. The main portrait is of the current incumbent of the Mangkunegaran seat.

Karsten's renovation of
the Mangkunegaran
palace updated the
bathroom. The Javanese
bathe using a dipper to
scoop out cool water from
a cistern, splashing it
over the body. Statuettes
of Chinese, European and
Javanese subjects
decorate this area,
seemingly in concert with
the Victorian statue of
Plenitude, above, at the
inner courtyard of the
Kraton Hadiningrat in
the same city.

Raden Adjeng Kartini
was born in 1879, the
daughter of the Bupati of
Jepara, an important
Pasisir port. A champion
of education for women
and the Javanese, her
death in childbirth at 25
cut short a promising
career. The house where
she grew up preserves a
heavy European look,
with wood panelling and
lace curtains.

The Kraton of Sultan
Hamengkubuwono in
Yogyakarta. The main
gateway, right, is a blind
passageway. While the
kraton is very much
oriented on a north-south
axis, views and vistas
running along this axis
are purposely avoided
within the kraton walls.
It would not be proper for
any straight passageway
to pierce the interior of
the kraton.

◆

The use of wrought-iron and mild-steel brackets to support eaves was seen by some early-20th-century architects as proof of the decadence of the neoclassical heritage of the preceding century. They are pleasing to today's tastes.
The use of strong colours for house walls, as at right, is particularly striking in the mosque districts of Pasisir cities.

The four-column veranda of this house on Java's North Coast conforms to the typical Indo-European pattern. Radically simplified columns of the Tuscan order support the main roof. Typically wooden or ironwork columns will support the large overhang extension. Swing doors are useful as a way of encouraging ventilation while blocking a direct view inside the house.

The generous scale and freely interpreted Beaux-Arts decoration add to the appeal of this Pasisir house. The art-nouveau stained-glass decoration dates the building to the turn of the century. In the gardens can be seen planters based on classic models; these are a common element in Java's tempo-doeloe *villas*.

◆

Victorian fretted eaveboards and lacy wrought-iron railings divide the front porch of the house from the street in an attractive Surabaya neighbourhood. The level of decoration on town houses like these makes walking through the old neighbourhoods of Java's cities an enjoyable experience.

—————◆—————

Deep shade and Java's intense sunlight form sharp contrasts: Java is not a place of misty moodiness! Above, the photograph captures a characteristic silhouette: the man at the centre wears a pici, the Muslim cap popularized in the early 20th century. The photograph left, also from Surabaya, marks the strength of noon-time light. The passenger in the becak, or passenger tricycle, will welcome shelter from the sun; the driver will receive the full force of the sun's rays.

♦

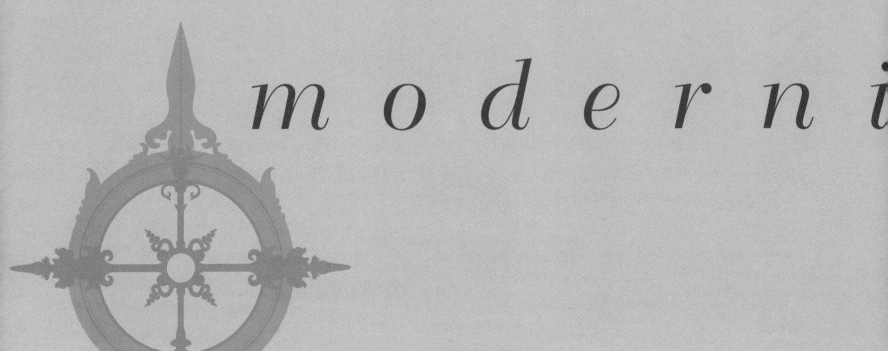

m o d e r n i

s m s

modernisms

In 1911 Java was enjoying a boom. Export prices were high, and European businesses were expanding into the countryside and smaller cities of Java. The future seemed bright, as the colonial government began to invest in education and local welfare under its new Ethical Policy. Then, shocking news spread. In districts of Surabaya and Semarang, the native population was falling ill of bubonic plague. This led to outrage, and less nobly, to acute embarrassment. How could such a medieval disease strike such a progressive colony? Measures had to be taken, and among them were new laws that outlawed attap and

Semarangan furniture in art-nouveau and art-deco designs was churned out by factories across Java in the first half of the century. Many pieces are still in use around the island.

bamboo for houses, for fear that they harboured rats and other vermin. City houses not built of masonry, with terracotta tiles or zinc roofing, the government announced, would be torn down.

From today's perspective it is remarkable that this programme was begun so reflexively, without the input of trained architects, and without even cursory study of the traditional Javanese architecture that was now to

be eradicated by government fiat. It must be remembered how colonial opinion held that local architecture had no value. In the words of a 1914 report "neither as regards size nor with a view to construction do the native buildings occupy a place of the slightest prominence in the architecture of the present time."

Years after the fact, the architect Henri Maclaine-Pont decried the attempt to impose new building types on a population, without reference to their existing styles: "the first results were disastrous...the building proscriptions, where introduced, made a drastic end to the characteristic building forms and methods." Most scholars agree that this regulation had a deep impact on Java, and the new regulations were widely followed.

For Javanese and Europeans alike in the first part of the 20th century, becoming modern was a vital imperative. Only by learning modern ways of science, technology, health, education, only by reforming and revitalizing Islam or Javanese tradition to respond to the challenges of the new era, could Java take its proper place in the world. This struggle, and this adventure, of being and becoming modern, has left its mark on Java Style.

In the early part of the 20th century, a host of styles in architecture and design arose in Europe to satisfy the need to be new: art nouveau, Viennese Secessionism, art deco, all of these expressed feelings of change, a rejection of the past. Later styles sought to express the impact of speed, motion, the machine. And all of these styles found a ready audience and expression in a Java that was facing its own time of great change. The new designs were most used for institutional buildings to meet the needs of a booming economy: hospitals, hotels, schools and technical colleges, factories, warehouses and office buildings.

So whether the builder was a colonial official out

to prove how progressive his colony was, or an Islamic educator who wanted to demonstrate that reformed Islam was legitimately modern, both drew on a common pool of design ideas and inspirations.

This striking house façade makes a decidedly carefree, art-deco -flavoured interpretation of classical forms, including columns, capitals and the open disk-topped pediment. The street-level decoration is decidedly austere compared to the second storey.

Among the European architects who were impor-tant bearers of new ideas, and who trained the first generation of modern Indonesian architects, two approaches emerged. One was synthetic and sensitive to Java's own vernacular and classical styles, seeking to create an Indo-European modern architecture. The other group of architects was much less interested in Java's past or its traditions. Architects like C.P. Wolff Schoemaker or A.F. Aalbers saw these as impediments. Their job was to build the most modern, the most impressive, the most smoothly functional buildings they could, as symbols of a Java improved by the application of the latest European principles, though perhaps incorporating detailing inspired by the 'classical' Hindu-Javanese past. And there was no more respect for the colonial neoclassical villa than there was for the

vernacular. One architect decried Indo-European hous-es as "insipid imitations of a soulless neo-Hellenism, bad copies of sad models, mute, white witnesses to a century of tastelessness and an inability to create." Distaste made him eloquent.

F.J.L. Ghijsels, was one of the most important of this second group of architects, who has left a rich archive of letters and drawings. He had little feeling for the art and design of Java. In a letter to his wife, he said of Yogyakarta, "you always get the feeling that everything is filthy and dirty. This is also because the natives dress in dark, colourless clothes, there are almost no cheerful colours in the jackets and *sarongs,* everything dark, sober, blue." That Yogya *batik* could leave someone as visually sensitive as Ghijsels cold is remarkable. It is an indication of the tentative nature of his own engagement with traditional Java.

Many of Ghijsels' buildings still survive, most notably the Kota railway station in north Jakarta, and many were in fact quite innovative and sensitive to the practical requirements of building in the tropics. He was an extremely talented architect, and after a pas-sage of years, you could say that his buildings have been 'reclaimed' by Java. Good architecture cannot help but be responsive to climate, to landscape, to the surroundings, no matter what the architect's ideology. And buildings are invested with importance by the uses they are put to, by their places in the daily lives of peo-ple who use them.

But two important architects sought to engage Java more actively. Thomas Karsten and Henri Maclaine-Pont had been classmates at the Delft Technological High School, one of the first institutions in Holland to train architects in both engineering and aesthetic principles. Maclaine-Pont was born in Indonesia, of an old colonial family. His career was a fascinating journey. His most famous work, the

The machine and the skyscraper, symbols of the new, in the floor decoration of the Hotel Niagara.

Institute of Technology Bandung, or ITB, was completed comparatively early in his career, in 1918. It still fulfils its function as the seat of one of Indonesia's premier educational institutions remarkably well, (Indonesia's first President, Soekarno, was among its first intake) and it stands out today as an important marker on the path to an Indonesian modern style. But for Maclaine-Pont the building was only a start. While he had managed to integrate Javanese and Sumatran design ideas into a modern building, he realized that he needed to learn more about the deep structural principles of the traditional architecture of Greater Sunda, as he termed the *nusantara*.

He joined the Civil Health Survey, in an attempt to find traditional solutions to the problems of pests and poor sanitation, so as to arrest the wholesale destruction of Java's traditional architecture in the name of modernization. He travelled and studied throughout Java and Sumatra, and in 1924 he became fascinated with Trowulan, the site of the ancient capital of Majapahit. He established an archeological foundation and architectural workshop there, investigating Majapahit remains while experimenting with stressed roof designs that applied Austronesian structural principles to modern materials. His goal? "To catch the interest of the people on a grand scale for the real sense of their forgotten modes of dwelling and building, at the same time demonstrating how the same principles could be used in modern times, with modern insight and eventually, as well, modern materials." The roof forms he developed, and his research, inspired later European theoretical works on roof structures.

Thomas Karsten's approach was more obviously cultural: in his designs for museums, performing arts centres, and in his renovations for the Mangkunegaran Palace in Solo he sought to identify designs that were in harmony with his ideas of Javanese culture. He was a sensitive observer, and in the case of the Mangkunegaran he had collaborated closely with the court. He knew enough to know that progress towards an integrated Javanese style, "based on the roots of an old culture but an expression of a new and completely young life," could only come about when the Javanese "educated, with expertise and awareness, take building into their own hands."

Karsten's main business was urban planning, and

Front porch and gate of a pre-war house: the cities of Java are dotted with neighbourhoods of houses like this, built in the 1930s under plans by Thomas Karsten and others.

plotting the growth of Semarang and Malang. Many of these suburbs are still intact, with their pleasant tree-lined, winding streets, and European-styled villas with high-peaked tile roofs. The house designs were a sharp departure from the neoclassical villas of the *tempo doeloe*. If the villas of the *tempo doeloe* were Javanese houses with European trim, the houses of Candi Baru and Menteng were European houses with Javanese characteristics. Some featured streamlined rooftop ornaments at the peak of steep, pyramidal roofs. Renditions of old Hindu motifs found their way into the façades and decorations of public buildings, and many buildings made sensible use of deep roof overhangs, verandas, airwells and open galleries aimed at maximizing ventilation.

The manufacture of furniture was one of the industries to undergo a spurt of growth at this time. Furniture in art-nouveau and art-deco designs and tropical woods was mass produced in factories in Surabaya and Semarang, following European fashions and utilizing screws and glues instead of traditional joinery. Today many such pieces are still around, and are known as 'Semarangan' style.

Part of the unique impact of Java Style on a foreign visitor is the way that early-20th-century modernisms are still so evident, in cities and in villages. Why?

For one thing, the great depression of the 1930s was devastating to Java, and was followed by years of war, revolution and struggle. This meant there was a hiatus in the development of Java Style. When in the

1950s Java as a part of a newly independent Republic of Indonesia began to search for ways to express itself, it quite sensibly turned to the Javanese art-deco style that had begun in the 1920s. This design sensibility was the root of the first Indonesian national style in the 1950s. Indonesia was spared the large-scale housing blocks of modernist brutalism: the new state was neither wealthy enough nor so arrogant as to impose this. The urban planners of Java's early independence, notably S. Soesilo, were ex-colleagues of Karsten's, and continued many of the principles that he had set out, providing a continuity from the 1930s to 50s.

Only when the pace of development began really to pick up in the 1970s under the New Order, when economic growth and foreign investment became watchwords, did late modern and postmodern styles replace the modernisms of the early 20th century. Glass and steel, air-conditioning and satellite dishes form the most widely accepted vocabulary of what it means to be up-to-date today.

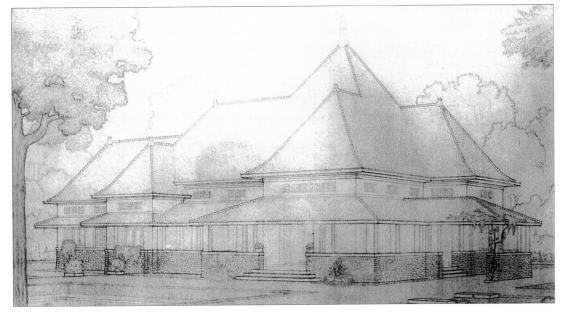

F.J.L. Ghijsels has left many wonderful drawings of his designs, including this 1925 luxury villa in Yogyakarta. The deep roof overhangs and large veranda make the house more comfortable in the heat, this and the roof finial help locate the design in Java.

The Oranje Hotel of
Surabaya was originally
opened in the 1900s.
The hotel was renovated
in 1993, and reopened as
the Hotel Majapahit.
Long cool corridors and
palm gardens recreate
the ideal of tropical
luxury that still has
a potent hold on
travellers to Java.

Café Batavia on
Fatahillah Square in
Kota in west Jakarta is
arguably Java's most
characterful nightspot.
Its decoration is an
eclectic mix of 19th-
century and art-deco
styles that succeeds in
capturing the feeling of
the old clubs that were
the focus of social life in
colonial times. The
sitting areas off the main
dining room (right) aim
for art-deco glamour; a
Chinese platform table
fits the mood nicely.

Oen's cake shops, the Toko Oen, are a fixture of Semarang, Surabaya and Malang in East Java. This Toko Oen, in Malang, preserves the feeling of fifty years ago. The Toko Oen serve Western food and cakes and sweets with a feeling of self-conscious novelty: they are reminders of a time when Western foods and fashions were exotic to Java. To today's generation of urban Indonesians the food and design style of the West are commonplace.

A *home in Malang, East Java, mixes a variety of early-20th-century elements. Stained-glass windows inspired by Frank Lloyd Wright lend a certain atmosphere to a room dominated by an older bed, the typical Victorian round marble-topped table, and cane love seat. The rocking chair is a rather ungainly type that was very popular in Java in the late 19th century.*

The cool blue-and-white floor tiles in this Malang house harmonize surprisingly well with the potted ferns and wooden furniture common to so many Javanese houses. The unpainted door surrounds, with geometricized pediments, and the wrought-iron grilles in the transom window are particularly attractive. The two dogs of Fu, traditionally placed in front of Chinese homes or temples, complete the pattern.

Spare, symmetrical and straightforward, these house façades are from Gresik, East Java. They display a confident use of coloured glass, cement floor tiles and brick trim. Bright colours are well suited to the tropical sunlight. The furniture (right) uses rattan to simulate upholstered cushions, in a style that has a Weiner Werkestatte simplicity. The art-deco pintu angin, or swinging doors, are a particularly attractive feature.

◆

The symmetry of this front gallery of a house in Yogyakarta is accentuated by two ornate cut-glass mirrors and matching stands on either side of the main door into the private areas of the house. Saloon doors — or pintu angin — are relatively common on Java: they preserve privacy while encouraging ventilation. This pair features Chinese woodcarving and stained glass; the combination catches the light to create a pleasing effect in the room further inside. A pressed-tin ceiling and cool, concrete floor tiles frame this particularly attractive combination.

◆

Further inside the house a stairway ascends; custom cabinet work creates storage space from the stairway voids (raised off the floor to minimize damaging dampness). The staircase features a particularly fine balustrade. The Thornet bentwood rocker completes the scene.

A *fine example of a traditional Javanese house updated with features and furniture of the early 20th century. Wooden dowels placed between the paired trusses of a Javanese roof frame mix well with the fretwork in this Javanese house in Kota Gede, outside Yogyakarta. The different heights of the spaces here indicate that this room is a* pringgitan, *the public semi-veranda leading to the interior. The platform at the left of the picture is equivalent to a* pendopo, *a place for receiving guests, with its less formal giant bamboo furniture.*

◆

This religious school outside Yogyakarta features an attractive, pared-down interpretation of traditional Javanese wood-frame construction. The forms of the pendopo can serve the needs of a modern school as well as the Javanese house. The light doors between the open pavilion and the interior of the school are also common to Javanese houses, just repeated here on a slightly larger scale.

This house in Kota Gede, Yogyakarta, expresses an identity which is self-consciously both Muslim and modern. Building schools and community centres was very much part of reformist Islam in Java in the first twenty years of the 20th century. The stars and stylized crescents on the doors were part of a design vocabulary that was common to reform Islam around the world.

The Menara Kudus Mosque is one of Java's most ancient mosques, with its Hindu-styled brick tower (see page 42). It finds its way into this chapter due to the quality of the renovation of 1930, which added a serambi, or porch for worshippers, floored in high-quality terrazzo, its arches framed with stained-glass panels combining art-deco motifs with the words of the Holy Al-Koran.

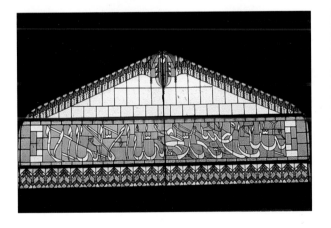 

The Hotel Niagara in Lawang, East Java, is set in the saddle between two volcanoes south of Surabaya, in a garrison town that also housed a popular sanitarium. The hotel, built by a Chinese entrepreneur, is an exotic, eccentric structure, designed in an art-nouveau style by a Brazilian architect some time after 1910. No expense was spared, and the quality of its detailing has survived many years of benign neglect. Superb terrazzo or 'Shanghai plaster' floors, mosaic tiling (like that spelling out the word 'Salve' or 'Welcome' at left), art-nouveau glazed tiles and wrought-iron balustrades are among the elements in this mix. The hotel was undergoing renovations at the time of photography. Now much of the original luxuriousness of its fittings is restored.

◆

Stained and etched glass in styles of the early part of this century survives in surprising quantities in Java. The quality of the craftsmanship is generally very high, and the level of detail often striking, as in the art-deco panel below right. Such panels are now part of the antique trade, and many impoverished households have sold off their original windows. The image top right is related only visually: these are the serving cups of a roadside pudding vendor.

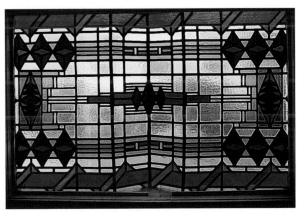

*O*n opening in 1921, the Technical College in Bandung was the first tertiary educational institution in Java. Henri Maclaine-Pont's design included massive roofs inspired by the traditional roofs of the nusantara, and the placement of buildings in the compound, linked by covered walkways and oriented towards the Tangkuban Perahu volcano, owes much to Java's kratons. The roof uses traditional wooden shingles, and natural stone forms the columns.

Today, the Bandung Technical College has become the Institut Teknologi Bandung or ITB, one of Indonesia's finest educational institutions. Its main ceremonial space is this public hall, its high-arched ceiling is supported by curved beams made of laminated wood reinforced with metal clamps. The building is highly successful, but Maclaine-Pont was dissatisfied, knowing that he had not captured the essence of the structural genius of the traditional architecture of the nusantara.

◆

The charm of the Hotel
Surabaya in Bandung
lies in its simplicity.
Its design is a stripped-
down art-deco classicism.
The hotel, on the pattern
of a large traditional
Javanese house, makes
much use of small
internal courtyards like
this one separating the
rooms from the shared
bathing area.

Coloured glass, in panels that make an art-deco play on verticals and rectangles, silhouettes a hotel staff member. Such moments make Java Style.

Detailing in Javanese homes and buildings of the early 20th century is generally excellent: the skill of Java's craftsmen extends beyond wood-carving or wayang puppet-making to mild steel, plasterwork and stained glass. The veranda opening on this art-deco house in Solo, central Java, frames the mossy outer wall: tropical weathering cannot be avoided; good designs will make use of the contrast between freshly painted surfaces and weathered outer walls.

◆

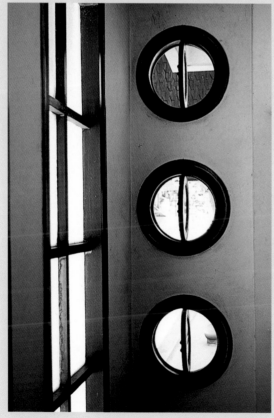

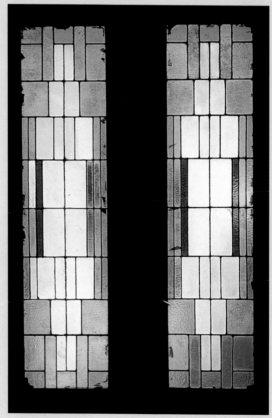

The Hotel Keprabon of Solo is a treasure trove of art-deco details executed in tropical hardwoods. Rooms are placed off the open corridor; patrons take tea or a simple breakfast outside their rooms, at tables and chairs set along the open hallway.

The stairway at the Hotel Keprabon is a minor masterpiece: note the curved swastika shapes in the balustrade. The asymmetries and strong verticals of the wooden doors are characteristic of Java deco; tea served in glasses with porcelain covers is a staple of simple hotels like this one.

◆

The Office of the Governor of West Java, far left, is one of the public buildings erected in Bandung at the time the Dutch government was considering moving the colony's capital to the city from Jakarta. Built by government architect J. Gerber in 1920, it was suitably designed for the tropics and makes liberal use of Hindu-Javanese inspired decoration. It is popularly known as the 'Gedung Saté', for the spheres on a stick that crown it. The City Hall of Cirebon, above, is nicknamed 'Balai Udang', or Shrimp Hall, for the crustacean motifs that adorn it. The Villa Isola, left, was designed by C.P. Wolff Shoemaker, and was built in 1933 for an eccentric Indo-European press baron.

The Savoy Homann
Hotel in Bandung
captures the transition
between art deco and a
more sober and massive
functionalism. Designed
in 1939 by A.F. Aalbers,
it was built at a time
when Bandung was
booming, and the Dutch
government was
considering whether to
move its capital here in
the highlands from the
heat of Jakarta. Aalbers
survived internment by
the Japanese, and
returned to Holland to
practise as an architect
after the war.

A *freewheeling interpretation of the Space Age, the Apotik Sputnik in Semarang on Central Java's North Coast captures a moment in time that seized the world's imagination. With its connotation of cleanliness and scientific efficacy, the Sputnik look would seem admirably suited to the functions of a pharmacy; the establishment's total design extends to the labels on its medicine bottles (lower right). Most impressive perhaps is the evident loving care with which Dra. S Brotosisworo has maintained his establishment over the years.*

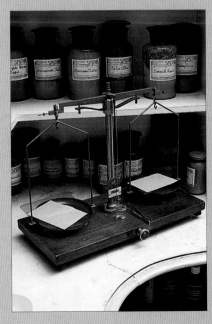

contem

porary

homes

contemporary homes

According to the old Javanese treatise on such matters, a man without a house of his own is like a plant that does not flower: besides not producing any fruit, the plant is unattractive and plain. After all, a house is the first of the five attributes of the Javanese gentleman: the other four are a wife, a *keris* or dagger, a songbird, and a horse.

When building a house in the Javanese heartland, there is one value that must be preserved above all. The house and its owner must be *cocok:* appropriate to each other, or fitting. Many things determine the appropriateness of a house and its owner. Ideally these elements reinforce each other, locking together like the posts and beams of a Javanese roof frame. The variables include the personality of the owner, his social status and family position, the orientation of the site, the day the building begins, the size of the house, the position of its various elements and their decoration.

As part of the effort to make sure house and owner are *cocok,* a traditional house is built around a unit of measurement that derives from the owner's own body. Some carpenters would traditionally use the space between the index fingers on hands joined at the tips of outstretched thumbs, to arrive at the *dim* or *kaki.* A variety of formulae yield the measurements of the house from this unit, ingeniously ensuring that the very tall or very short do not get houses which stand out too much from the norm. In designing a house, relative proportion is everything.

The idea of showing off is antithetical to traditional Javanese ideals. Humility is seen as a sign of depth, part of the self-control that is considered a key mark of refinement. Consequently, the style of traditional Java is not exuberant. It is understated, subtle, perhaps even a bit shabby, in the manner of an impoverished aristocrat unconcerned with making an impression.

*The front veranda or semi-*pendopo *of the Jaya Ibrahim house in West Java. The house makes a free, confident reference to both the great tradition, and the neoclassical, colonial past. As well, the designer has drawn on his own taste for Venetian and Moorish architecture to form a unique new creation.*

Never in Javanese history have courts and palaces manipulated scale to impress. Palaces are larger than homes, but not excessively so. The arrangements of the many buildings within the palace are, however, carefully modulated: gates and doorways are placed with calculated effect, as one moves deeper and deeper into the centre of the magical realm which is the *kraton*.

Traditional Java retains a number of ideas of how spatial order must harmonize with a greater one. While many contemporary Javanese of a particularly secular or Islamic bent might reject this, there is still in Java today a rich sense of the numinous, of powerful forces that are beyond the mundane. Javanese tradition preserves a great many ideas of how these forces are to be dealt with in the manner and timing of design and construction of a home. Whether to follow the customary guidelines or not, whether to do so in detail or with a cursory nod, is a decision which a Javanese would have to make, as a contemporary Chinese in Hong Kong or Singapore must decide whether or not to worry about the principles of *feng-shui* or geomancy.

The process of finding a style appropriate to the end of the 20th century on Java is an intriguing one, offering plenty of ways to go astray. In Jakarta and Surabaya today, as in most of booming Asia, the expressive vigour of wealth abounds. Houses are built up to the edge of property lines, maximizing the use of increasingly expensive land. Today, Madam de Wit's question of life in Java—"How to keep cool?"—is answered emphatically: "With air conditioning!"

Will Java Style end in this? In massive houses, presenting blind walls and reflective glass to the streets, totally reliant on *ahsay*, or air-conditioning, and topped off with parabola, satellite dishes that can span three, four, or even five yards? Probably not. Despite the insecurity, even aggression manifested in such houses,

there are encouraging signs that Java Style is capable of responding to the challenges of new wealth and new lifestyle pressures. Only the most crass among the newly

This restaurant, in East Java uses a pendopo *raised on a platform over an enclosed set of rooms, allowing an open space above or an air-conditioned one below.*

wealthy fail to show an appreciation for the antiques and antiquities of Java and for the splendid output of Java's fine artists. The excellent work of a new generation of resort hotel designers working in Southeast Asia, especially Bali, has inspired many with a new idea of luxury, one based on the sensual possibilities of the tropical climate, and design heritage of traditional cultures.

If there is one home which encompasses the possibilities of Java Style at the end of the 20th century, it is the home, studio and workshop of Kanjeng Raden Temenggung Hardjonegoro, in Solo. An official of the Kraton Surakarta Hadiningrat, an expert on its ways and ceremonials, an acclaimed court dancer, K.R.T. Hardjonegoro is most famous as one of Indonesia's foremost *batik* artists. From the road his home appears to be a tidy 1950s late-art-deco house, but upon entering through a side gate, the visitor finds quite a different realm, in a compound of several buildings in the plot behind the house. The host receives his guests on the terrazzo-floored streamline-curved back porch of the original house, around a neoclassical pedestal table accompanied by fine Raffles chairs. To the south stands the *pendopo*, originally built in Semarang, where Prince Puger was crowned Paku Buwono I. Classical statuary collected from Central Javanese villages, and now donated to the Indonesian government, is set in niches around the courtyard. To the west, beyond a wall graced with bougainvillea is the airy *batik* studio, with its cool concrete floor and its walls of woven bamboo, taking the very best from Javanese village vernacular.

In its mix of neoclassical, art deco, the village and court traditions of Java, the home is a summation of the way that Java Style can connect with the past, and so forge a deep sense of place. In the way the house celebrates this mixed heritage, and in its use of the textures of rock and gravel to contrast with plaster and greenery, it could only be a late-20th-century creation, inseperable from the particular sensibility of its owner.

Iwan Tirta is another of Java's *batik* pioneers, acknowledging the skills and values of the best of old *batik* while adapting the form to the new uses of a modern lifestyle, in fashion and furnishings. In keeping with his focus, more tuned to the lifestyles of modern Jakarta, Iwan Tirta's own house deploys the furnishings of a Javanese noble house—antique porcelains, traditional *lemari* or cupboards and court portraits in oils—

in spaces that are common to cosmopolitan urbanites the world over. A similar approach can be seen in Hudi Suharnoko's apartment in Jakarta. He has assembled a collection of paintings, Majapahit carvings and bronzes, as well as old furniture, and created a style that we might call 'Old Java'. Here colours, textures and objects reflect a deep pride in Java's civilization, though it is probably fair to add that this is a pride that looks on somewhat from a distance.

A recent trend in the antique market was the taste for the so-called 'Java primitive'. In East Java, villagers often make creative use of odd pieces of teak, too weathered or irregular to adapt to other uses. With the strategic application of a leg here, a bit of trimming there, these pieces are transformed into *amben* or benches. Their monolithic character, and their expression of the qualities of wood seems suited to modern taste. The house of artist Teguh Ostenrijk (pages 188–89) displays a particularly good piece.

In the 1950s and 60s, the idea of the fine modern home in Jakarta was a continuation of the European villas of the 1930s, one that could have been as well built in Wassenar in Holland as Indonesia. But beginning in the 1970s, where space allowed, a few adventurous home owners attempted to design houses that drew directly on the traditional Javanese experience of space. Many have re-used old Javanese buildings, particularly *pendopo*, or parts of buildings, to create this new and adventurous hybrid.

Perhaps the first such house in Jakarta was built by Admiral Subiyakto, ex-Chief of Staff of the Indonesian Navy. His house lies in a brick-walled compound, combining several buildings. A gate (pictured on pages 164–65) opens directly onto the road, and the visitor passes through a courtyard, and an entrance pavilion, before coming into a second

Contemporary tastes have come to appreciate the raw, monumental look of wooden furniture and utensils from villages in East Java. Benches, plates and serving bowls are often simply carved out of great blocks of teak.

144

courtyard in front of a large *pendopo,* which leads to a last, quasi-*pendopo* built up against the rear wall of the compound. A superb Kudus door is mounted on this wall, forming a backdrop for the sitting room. Bedrooms and service areas are built to the side of the main axis. While a large Kudus door was incorporated into the design of the Kudus Bar at Jakarta's Hilton Hotel in the mid-1970s, marking the first use of an important element of a Javanese house in a modern interior, the Subiyakto house uses the old door or screen in a setting that is strikingly original, and one that is a direct reference to Javanese spaces.

A more recent, and very adventurous use of an old *pendopo* is the house of Bambang Supriadi. Here a large Solo *pendopo* has been raised up to such a height that an entire floor can be inserted underneath. The floor of the *pendopo* space is now, unusually, made of wood (for traditional *pendopo* are built on the ground). The rooms underneath the raised *pendopo* are brick-walled, relatively small and air-conditioned, in contrast to the *pendopo* space above, which is open to all the effects of climate and weather.

In Europe and America, Java Style is having its own impact, mostly through Javanese furniture, especially the rustic neoclassical. Colonial armchairs turn up in the pages of interior magazines with some regularity. An appreciation for the Javanese approach to space and the tropical environment is also spreading internationally, much of it by way of Bali. David Bowie's house in Mustique, designed by Bali-based Linda Garland, is an example of this new internationalized Java Style.

The latest, and perhaps most confidently adventurous of the important new homes in Java, is the house of Jaya Ibrahim near Bogor, an hour or two's drive into the hills south of Jakarta. It is thoroughly postmodern, with Venetian and Moorish references, and making use of simple, locally sourced materials. The overall effect is

These brackets, on the Jaya Ibrahim house, are simply updated versions of wrought-iron examples of the 19th century. They are light and graceful, more decorative than load-bearing.

a cool, streamlined style that manages to use the past in a fresh, contemporary manner. The house draws on the same experience of space which the old Indo-European houses enjoyed: views and vistas from the veranda. Here these vistas are superb, of the garden and over the hills to Mt. Salak, the same volcano which featured in so many colonial prints and paintings of Bogor (such a painting inspired the owner's search for land here).

And so, in the same way a pilgrim ends a circum-ambulation of the Borobudur temple, we end with a view of the landscape, towards the volcano. In its various meanings and manifestations, in the houses of Java's wealthy and her artists, in the simple homes of Java's villages, and in the homes built by foreigners inspired by this island, Java Style will always point towards to the volcano. The design heritage of Java, which this book has sketched in only the briefest of outlines, is inseparable from the matchless landscape and the deep-seated natural (and dare we say spiritual) forces that brought this island into being.

Displaying a confident use of the design of the past, the front veranda of the Jaya Ibrahim house is furnished with Javanese antique furniture. Its square plan is reminiscent of a pendopo, *but its ornament, masonry columns, balustrade, furnishings, staircase approach, and relation to the large landscaped garden tie it more directly to the tradition of the veranda of the Indo-European house.*

The front veranda is dominated by two kursi gobang, *reclining chairs with double arms, one element of which can swing out to receive the outstretched legs of the reclining person.* Kursi *comes from the Persian for 'chair'.* Gobang *was the name for a coin used to fasten the armrest or leg-rest to the pivot. Such chairs became popular in the second half of the 19th century.*

The pointed arches on the balcony in the interior view above are a Moorish touch to the Jaya Ibrahim house. Floor-to-ceiling louvred doors on tracks are becoming very popular in new Jakarta houses: they update the older hinged Javanese door screens. The column capital echoes but does not imitate Javanese carpentry. Flanking the doorway on the facing page are two candle stands, crucial items of furniture in 19th-century households.

The colours and textures of the batik, old Dutch silver and kitchen Ming plates, and the palm-leaf wrapping for ketupat *rice cakes harmonize well in this table setting, left, at the Jaya Ibrahim house. The* kawung, *or interlocking circle pattern of the* batik *used as a tablecloth is echoed in the tinted concrete floor designs of the house, seen on preceding pages.*

◆

In keeping with the eclectic nature of the house, combinations of diverse objects give a rich sense of intimacy to the guest bedroom: Majapahit tuff and terracotta accompany European blue-and -white tablewear and old brass on the bedside tables. The owner's bedroom is decorated with old architectural plans, and uses the sheen of silk and stressed metal textures to contrast with rich earthy tones elsewhere.

Classical statues, including the elephant-headed Hindu god Ganesha, lend a certain air to the compound of K.R.T. Hardjonegoro in Solo, Central Java. They have been donated to the Indonesian state. Whitewashed walls dazzle in the spectacular Javanese sunlight; deep shadows, bougainvillea and volcanic-stone floors lend balance.

◆

An oasis just off a busy road in Solo, the K.R.T. Hardjonegoro house reflects the interests of the owner as a one-man repository of knowledge of traditional Java. Visible in the photograph below is a fine Pasisir pendopo from Semarang, rescued from demolition in Solo. The main house can be seen at left, the batik studio at right. The photograph above shows the walls of the batik studio, plus another outbuilding.

At the time it was built, the Hardjonegoro residence was one of the first to innovate in the mixture of old Javanese house forms in new combinations. It also houses some important pieces of antique furniture, including the old VOC chair above, and the palanquin. The view right needs little elaboration: K.R.T. Hardjonegoro sits at the table where he receives his guests on the rear veranda.

K.R.T. Hardjonegoro's batik *makers work in a simple but richly textured building with walls of woven bamboo; they are known for having the finest hands in Java. The* loro blonyo *set at left would be traditionally placed in front of the house altar. This set is one of the finest known from the late 19th century; the photos capture the elegance of the back view.*

The house of Guruh
Soekarnoputra on Jalan
Sriwijaya in Jakarta was
built in a 1950s modern
style much loved by the
current owner's father,
Indonesia's first
President, Soekarno.
Yet it incorporates the
Javanese traditional
senthong (a kind of
extended altar of three
small rooms) at the heart
of the house. Set inside
the central senthong here
is a fine krobongan, a
kind of altar or symbolic
throne, full of bolsters in
Indian patola cloth.
Pairs of objects,
including a loro blonyo
set, flank the entrance to
the senthong tengah.
A typical syncretic
Soekarno touch is the
addition of Balinese
statuettes atop the
columns of the senthong.
The house was built by
President Soekarno for
his wife Fatmawati.

Yale-trained lawyer turned batik artist, Iwan Tirta is one of modern Indonesia's cultural heroes. The spectacular bed is actually an old krobongan, or shrine canopy, with extremely fine carving. Notable is the fine batik bedspread of Iwan Tirta's own design, its motifs picked out and highlighted with light quilting. Such quilting of batik came into fashion in Jakarta in the late 1980s, started by a group of Americans resident in Jakarta.

Iwan Tirta's house draws on the furnishings of Central Java's court culture, including ancestral portraits in oil. The traditional lemari or armoire at the end of the room (top) features a heavily carved openwork pediment and two vertical eye-shaped medallions in the doors. Left, a fine loro blonyo pair in front of a traditional Balinese painting, placed on a Chinese table: a small sample of the eclectic qualities which Java Style can encompass.

A *traditional Balinese painted* ider-ider *(or valance) harmonizes extremely well with the white tuff-stone carvings of Majapahit and ancient bronzes (right). The living room of the Hudi Suharnoko apartment, above, also features an excellent old Javanese* lemari *with cabriole legs, which work together with the paintings, sculptures and VOC bench to form a warm, rich look redolent of history.*

Further variations on the warm, rich style of the Suharnoko house: Cambodian antique silver, ivory and a portrait of Indonesia's first President—a gift from President Soekarno to the family. The screen is classic Jepara. Below, two white tuff-stone models of houses with masonry walls are flanked by a relief and a bronze-footed holy-water vessel, all in Majapahit styles.

◆

Central Javanese batiks
are hung on the frame of
an old Javanese four-
poster bed. Cambodian
silver and an old
woodcarving ensure that
the bedside table enhances
the whole. Above is a
white tuff bust in
Majapahit style: the
elegant features and
flowing coiffure of the
model give an indication
of the sensual
sophistication of
Majapahit art.

A progression of spaces in the generously sized compound of the Subiyakto family. Brick and whitewash harmonize well with the gardens outside and the rich woodcarving inside, just visible in this view, but examined in more detail on the pages which follow. Admiral Subiyakto was among the first house owners in Indonesia to build new structures that incorporated a taste for tradition.

◆

Urban necessities place
the pendopo at the very
back of the Subiyakto
house compound, reached
by layered courtyards and
walkways. Column bases
are tall, in a Cirebon
style. The Regency
pedestal table—its top
a single piece of wood—
preserves its original feet,
claws with metal wheels.
The geese are Madurese,
once placed in front of a
kobrongan. Elsewhere is a
four-poster bed, above, in
a vigorous country style.

A steep roof over the veranda creates a double-storeyed space outside the main house. Rough stone flooring sets off the East Javanese benches and dowry chest. The rustic feeling is continued inside this house by the liberal use of garden cuttings. The Javanese floor mats seen at right have long been favoured as a means of keeping cool. The large country table is covered with an East Javanese indigo batik and local copperware. Terracotta, tuff and wood textures feature at right.

The interior of this house draws on wider sources than simply Java. This room features musical instruments from Borneo hung as decorative objects. The tough rattan and bark-cloth floor covering is from the same island. The chair is rustic Java; the seat of the chair, an imitation of Windsor models, is carved from a solid piece of wood.

◆

The setting of this
hillside house increases
the sense of being
surrounded by greenery
(top). In the veranda
dining area is a superb
classic East Javanese
country table meja lurah,
the desk of the village
head, its Dutch influence
evident in the roundels
at the top of each
remarkable leg.
Large bamboo chick
blinds shelter the area
during heavy rain.

The textures of unfinished teakwood, terracotta, tarnished bronze and iron are favourite ones for modern-day collectors of Javanese antiques. These images were all taken from the Widodo house in Malang, East Java. On this page is a collection of betel nut cutters in animal and bird forms, usually made of welded iron, with occasional inlaid silver or gold trim. Blacksmithing in Java is considered an art, producing in addition to the famous keris or dagger, implements like the betel cutters and the knife on the facing page.

Bronze figures and vessels (facing page, bottom left) have been produced continuously in Java since ancient days, and are highly collectible. The Javanese souvenir industry has been churning out figures like those at top on the facing page for decades, some of which have rather a great deal of charm.

◆

In the Supriyadi house,
a Solo pendopo, dismant-
led, moved and rebuilt in
Jakarta, has been raised
so high that brick-walled
rooms have been inserted
underneath. The walls
mix open-carved trans-
oms, wood panels, frame
windows and panels of
woven bamboo.
The image at top
juxtaposes the back of a
village bench with a
carved panel. Details of
the tumpang sari carving
can be seen above.

The Supriyadi house mixes open pendopo spaces above and enclosed brick rooms at the lower level, which can be air-conditioned. The ground floor bedroom has a sliding glass door, and features a fine 18th-century bed, covered in a bedspread made of Madurese batik. Above the bed hangs a warp ikat textile from Savu, an island in the eastern archipelago of Indonesia. A large Madurese chest sits at the foot of the bed.

A *Chinese balustraded opium bed, made of two halves joined together, and a painting by Suparto are the chief features of the lower-storey room, left. Above, a veranda faces a wall of greenery, furnished with two plain teak chairs of neoclassical inspiration, a large Javanese* lemari, *an unusual marble-topped table and the ubiquitous Raffles bench.*

The Onghokam house, belonging to one of Indonesia's foremost historians. Top, a simple limasan *roof shelters an open dining area with Regency-inspired village benches. Above, the study is protected by a screen door. Right, the carved bamboo inscription and celadon plates reflect the owner's Chinese ancestry. The chairs are locally made art nouveau, set at either side of a tea table in the formal pattern beloved by Chinese.*

This South Jakarta house was one of the earliest to make use of a variety of linked structures (and swimming pool) set within a large house compound. Many of the spaces, like the study above, are sealed and air-conditioned, however the textures of brick, wood and whitewash help maintain a continuity between the inside and outside. The owner's superb collection of antique is featured prominently throughout the house.

Masks for dancers of the tales of the wayang look down on an old Javanese four-poster at left. The dining room above places Javanese wayang golek puppets in front of a mirror, framed with gilded carving. The theatrical effect provides a commentary on the parties at table. Lacquered containers and bowls complement the rich tones of the wooden furniture.

This is the house of an artist: perhaps it would not be too difficult to guess that from the highly individual choice of objects here (as in the puppets, drawings and miniature sculptures above). Choreographer and painter Bagong Kussudiardjo has been in this house for many years, part of a compound of art and dance studios, rehearsal spaces, and galleries in Yogyakarta. The star attraction of the green, shady veranda is a bench on yet another Javanese variation of a Regency design (usually seen upholstered in its English incarnation). Hanging from the ceiling are bird cages, cow bells, decorated gourds, containers of incised bamboo, on the right of the picture, sculptures from Irian Jaya.

♦

Asmoro Damais is a batik designer based in Jakarta. The paintings in the living room, left, contribute to the airy, sophisticated feeling of this room, a gallery and living space. Batiks cover the working surface of the table, the bust on the side table is a copy of a famous central Javanese piece. Excellent use has been made of the narrow passageway, seen in two views at top right. Bamboo, outdoor furniture, brick paving and two stone Fu dogs heighten the drama of the passageway that ends in the trellis around Asmoro's veranda. A pleasant, dense garden feeling is achieved even though the house is located in the middle of busiest Jakarta, surrounded by traffic. Inside, a striking Madurese carved bed is given a canopy of textiles; old glass paintings surround the bedside table.

◆

A 1991 house in Jakarta achieves a striking modern Islamic tropical look. Carved screens separate the spaces of the house, and a series of three pointed arches separates the sitting room from the swimming pool. A small tiled pool adds a touch of the Alhambra to the room. The geometric ornament in the specially commissioned wood panels is derived from the endless-knot tile motif found in the Mantingan mosque. The themes of the endless knot and the pointed arch are repeated throughout the house, sometimes on a smaller scale.

◆

The Teguh Ostenrijk
house and gallery in
South Jakarta feature a
cool minimal look that
suits the artist's own
work. In the front, right,
is an East Javanese
village bench, a single
massive piece of wood.
Cushions and split
bamboo matting surround
a Chinese coffee table in
a stripped paint finish.
The dining room features
four kursi koboi, or
cowboy chairs, made from
roughly carved, extremely
dense teak wood along the
sides of the table.

Ardyanto is a batik
artist and painter living
outside Yogyakarta in
Central Java. His batiks
are exuberant fine-art
pieces. He also produces
pieces for furnishings,
like the tablecloth in the
foreground here.
The living and dining
room features an unlikely
combination of a densely
carved Kudus tumpang
sari with chandeliers,
cloth sashes, sashes of
pandan leaves, and
canopies.

◆

Ardyanto's study pairs a pleated canopy with traditional wood carving; a Dutch art-nouveau lamp hangs from its centre. The personal areas of the house are crammed full of objects collected by the artist — old bronzes, terracottas, a Memphis lamp, an African fetish, awards given to the artist, Chinese porcelains, jasmine pot-pourri — all collected on his frequent travels, and somehow harmonized, within Ardyanto's exuberant style.

Pastel colours and
murals by the artist
—of chintz-inspired
florals and floating
figures—combine with a
fine, large loro blonyo to
create a moment of magic
in the Ardyanto house.
Murals like this were not
uncommon in old
Javanese villas. The
cabinet is painted in
imitation of European
marquetry work.

One of Indonesia's style leaders is Josephine Kumara, proprietor of Bin House in Jakarta. Marshalling the products of a network of Java's most talented batik makers and weavers, Bin House is a gallery and workshop in an old bungalow in central Jakarta. This is the place to go for the very finest in contemporary Indonesian textiles, cloths that are highly innovative yet totally respectful of the skills and traditions of Indonesia's textile artists. Batik on silk feature in the images at left. In the view at right a large brass spittoon is used to hold a dramatic flower arrangement: the bold shapes of halyconia flowers are not native to Java, but they are becoming more and more popular among gardeners and flower arrangers. An old Chinese rice jar supports a tray holding a similar bouquet near the window. The bungalow's original cement tiles imitate terrazzo: they are equally cool. An unusual wooden settee completes the scene.

◆

Jaya Ibrahim's first house outside Jakarta has a cool, clean look inspired by Sir Edwin Luytens. The bedroom, below, with a Philippine nara wood desk, features an excellent collection of old glass paintings depicting characters from the wayang. Strong vertical lines everywhere accentuate the airy, spacious quality of the rooms. Polished terrazzo floors add to the impression of coolness.

Vertical grills provide security while contributing to the overall spare approach of Jaya Ibrahim's first house in Jakarta. In this view a quirky variation on a neoclassical couch displays some virtuoso caning. The large jar which flanks the brass lamp is called a Martaban jar or dragon jar. These glazed pots often feature dragon motifs, and were originally made in Burma and traded to Borneo and Java over the last three hundred years. This hallway is decorated with botanical prints, and terrazzo-like concrete floor tiles complete a cooling ensemble. A trademark of Jaya Ibrahim's style is his ability to use simple materials, easily available on Java and familiar to Javanese craftsmen, to achieve an impressive luxurious look.

◆

javane

se design

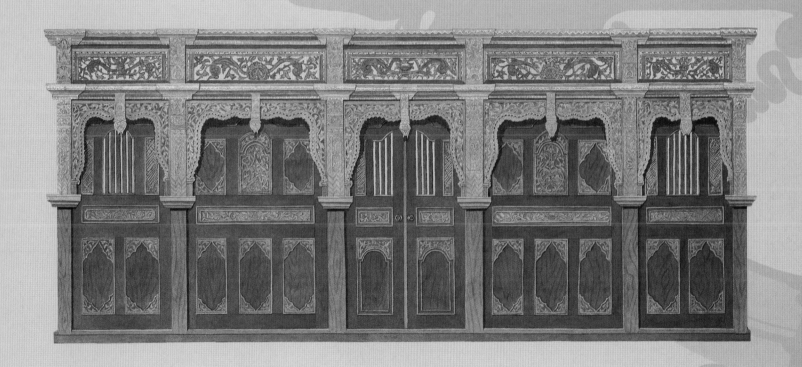

traditions

Until the 19th century, for the most part, the Javanese had little use for chairs. The words for chair and table in Javanese and Indonesian come from the European languages, reflecting their association with these new residents of Java. Most traditional pieces of Javanese furniture then are smaller objects, used for storage, or for specific ceremonial or personal use. Large platforms, some built into the frame of the house, served for sleeping, as did rattan mats.

Small wedding chests like this are common in Madura, but are possibly a Chinese import. They are used to carry valuables, traditionally as part of a wedding procession. A pole is inserted through the round holes at either end, one person takes each end of the pole, and the chest is airborne.

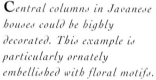

This is an ani-ani, a small knife used to cut rice stalks by hand (see page 20). The blade is inserted into the horizontal wing structure. The figure is surely that of Dewi Sri, the rice goddess. This piece was collected in the 1930s on the North Coast.

The Javanese martial tradition motivates some families to display weapons in their family collection, some of which might be heirlooms. Simple stands like this are appropriate for displaying spears, many of which will have blades welded of nickel and iron in complex patterns similar to keris blades. Keris holders, wall-mounted carved-wood plaques are also common items of furniture.

Central columns in Javanese houses could be highly decorated. This example is particularly ornately embellished with floral motifs.

This is a large day bed that would also be used to store valuables, including rice. This piece dates to the early 19th century, and bears carving of the Dutch coat of arms. Day beds such as this would have been for the first son to sleep on.

This oil lamp casts a shadow of a wayang figure, carved from wood. Wayang *figures* appear on other pieces of furniture and decoration, including kris *holders*, and carved wooden panels that are sometimes hung on either side of the entrances to old Javanese homes.

In Javanese architecture, column capitals and pillar bases are often adorned and carved. In many cases they are painted and gilded; today's taste is to leave them unpainted, to admire the colour of the wood.

This *vanity chest was a popular item of furniture in 18th-century Batavia, and examples similar to this can be found throughout the Pasisir or coastal regions of Java, Sumatra, and Borneo.*

This *pyramidal set of stacked boxes was used in Batavia in the mid-19th century for medicines. Its ornate carving and gilding, a seeming mix of Chinese, Balinese and European forms mark it as a creation of the Pasisir. Such boxes were also popular in other cosmopolitan Pasisir cities, like Palembang in South Sumatra, or Banjarmasin in South Kalimantan.*

Loro blonyo *figures, depicting the deity Dewi Sri and her consort Raden Sadono, are traditionally placed before the altar in the central altar room of a Javanese dwelling. There is wonderful regional variation in the styles of these pieces. Kneeling figures are usually from noble households.*

Another *Javanese piece, this betel nut set is crafted from brass and the shell of a coco-de-mer, a kind of double-lobed coconut that grows in the Seychelles islands in the Indian Ocean. Nuts from this tree sometimes wash up on the Indian Ocean (or as some say, the Indonesian Ocean) shorelines in Sumatra and Java. They are much prized.*

batavia

The style of Old Batavia was ornate and rich, created by the marriage of 17th- and 18th-century European tastes, and Indian, Chinese, and local skills (most of the cabinet-makers on the records of Batavia were Chinese). Non-European communities of Batavia had their own particular blend. Indian furniture was particularly influential in the early colonial period, and the finest tropical hardwoods (mahagony, amboyna and ebony) were favoured over teak.

A Batavia original: the burgomaster's chair, probably based on Indian models.

A Chinese bed: many kobrongan shrine canopies have decoration that resembles these carved panels.

Large chests were standard issue for colonial traders who moved goods by sea. In old Batavia, different officer grades were allowed chests of different sizes. Nineteenth century models were often placed on wheels.

A magnificent early-18th-century carved screen now in the collection of the Jakarta History Museum. Built for the East India Company's council room in Batavia, the screen depicts Pallas Athena after the defeat of Medusa, and carries the Seals of the council members in its crest.

*F*ine large cupboards were often left with unadorned doors, if the quality of the wood allowed. In the 19th century, openwork pediments became popular additions to large cupboards, especially in European and Javanese styles. This piece displays both characteristics.

*F*our-poster beds were once a necessity in Java: the frame allowed textiles and netting to be hung to counter mosquitos. Headboards often had openwork pediments, and turned dowels were the most frequently seen balusters.

*J*ava's Chinese community counted among their number many cabinetmakers, who produced furniture for a variety of customers. They also manufactured and imported furniture in Chinese styles. In particular, ornately carved narrow tables like this were used in front of large altars.

*C*arved wooden panels and screens find many uses in Java's houses—as dividers, inset into the large folding doors that filter public from semi-private spaces, and as decoration. Java absorbed carving styles from around the region, China and India.

neoclassical

A *modern variation on a common 19th-century armchair*

English furniture design of the early 19th century has had a lasting impact on Javanese furniture design, at all levels. Regency designs in particular became popular, well suited to the hardwood and rattan caning combination that was so comfortable in the heat, and which took advantage of locally available materials. Judging from the photographs which colonial officers took of themselves in their new homes, the standard issue furniture for government servants included Raffles chairs and recliners.

An early version of this Regency settee design can be found in the Jakarta History Museum, with the metal-wheeled feet characteristic of the period. In Europe, such settees were usually very richly upholstered in golden or red velvet: but this tropical version in rattan caning has proven very popular in Java.

Neoclassical forms are also followed in the 'village headman's table' from the teak plantation areas of the North Coast and East Java. The tables are often a little stolid, with legs that swell into large bulbous shapes before ending in small feet. This example has been modified on the instruction of an antique dealer to be used as a desk.

The plain curve of the pediment of this lemari *or cabinet contrasts with the ornamentation of the base and the cabriole legs.*

The Raffles chair: *Javanese versions of this basic Regency shape emphasise the flare of the chair back.*

The kursi gobang, *or planter's chair, with double swinging armrests that can support the recliner's outstretched legs, is found with cane and timber seats.*

Pedestal tables were a staple of interiors in Europe from the 18th century. Small ones were usually covered with tablecloths in lace or heavier textiles.

The Victorian marble-topped table is common throughout Southeast Asia.

This very common 19th-century armchair is inspired by Greek classical models.

The village bench based on Regency forms comes from the teak plantation areas of Java, where it was made in generous proportions, allowing it to be used as a bed, and allowing people to sit on it cross-legged. Village benches like this are perhaps the most striking example of the syncretic tastes one finds so often in Java. Cushions are modern additions.

205

modern designs

The late 19th and early 20th centuries were times of booming growth for Java. New factories in Semarang, Batavia and Surabaya began to produce furniture in the latest European styles, and for the first time architects began to specify the furniture to accompany their buildings. But whatever the style, there was no improving on the materials of Java's tropical setting: teak and other hardwoods and rattan caning.

Large hanging kerosene lamps have remained popular in Java since the Victorian era. Today the lamps are converted to receive electrical fittings, and new lamps are produced to the old design in order to satisfy the market's interest.

A vanity that combines lacy trim and delicate vertical members.

An art-nouveau-inspired design, this particular chair is very popular in Java.

The becak chair is based on the art-deco-style 1920s pedicabs, the sweeping curve of the armrest matching the curve of a bicycle wheel. Carpenters in Batavia built these for the front porches and verandas of town dwellings, and they have remained popular ever since.

Three-sided screens in a variety of styles are common on Java, often blocking front entrances so as to cut down on glare and afford privacy. Gothic-revival folding screens were very popular; this fixed screen has a Victorian feel to it. Coloured pebbled glass is inset into the wooden construction.

Art-nouveau-styled furniture was often left unpainted, with the appeal of the wood remaining. A way of lifting the design was to insert a glazed tile into the chair back. Such tiles were imported from Holland, France the UK and Japan, and were often added to the façades of shophouses.

This is a Beidermeier-inspired version of an Empire chair, which streamlines older neoclassical forms. The use of three vertical slats in the armrests is a popular cliché of Javanese furniture (it appears on three of the designs on this page).

suggested reading

Susan Abeyasekere, *Jakarta: A History*, Oxford University Press: Singapore 1987

Huib Akihary, *Architectuur & Stedebouw in Indonesië 1870/1970*, De Walburg Pers: Zuphen 1990

Huib Akihary, et al., *Ir F.J.L. Ghijsels: Architect in Indonesia (1910-1929)*, translated by T Burrett, Seram Press: Utrecht 1996

John Bastin & Bea Brommer, *Nineteenth Century Prints and Illustrated Books of Indonesia*, Spectrum Publishers: Utrecht 1979

Louis Couperus, *The Hidden Force*, translation revised and edited by E. M. Beekman, Library of the Indies, University of Massachusetts Press: Amherst 1985; first published in Dutch as *De Stille Kracht*, L.J. Veen: Amsterdam 1900; first English translation by Alexander Teixeira de Mattos, published by Jonathan Cape: London 1927

Soedarmadji JH Damais, editor, *Gedung Balai Kota Jakarta*, Pemerintah DKI Jakarta: Jakarta 1996

Jacques Dumarçay, *Histoire de l'Architecture de Java*, Publications de l'Ecole Française d'Extrême-Orient: Paris 1993

Jacques Dumarçay, *The House in South-East Asia*, Images of Asia, Oxford University Press: Kuala Lumpur 1987

Helen Ibbitson Jessup, *Court Arts of Indonesia*, The Asia Society Galleries in association with Harry Abrams: New York 1990

Helen Jessup, Four Dutch Buildings in Indonesia, in *Orientations* magazine, XIII, 9–12, 1982, Orientations: Hong Kong 1982

Koentjaraningrat, *Javanese Culture*, Institute of Southeast Asian Studies & Oxford University Press: Singapore 1985

Rob Nieuwenhuis *Tempo doeloe—een verzonken wereld, Fotografische documenten uit het oude Indië 1870–1920*, 3 volumes, [vol. 1] *Baren en oudgasten*, [vol. 2] *Komen en blijven*, [vol. 3] *Met vreemde ogen*, Em. Querido's Uitegeverif B.V., Amsterdam [vol. 1] 1981, [vol. 2] 1982, [vol. 3] 1988

Thomas Stamford Raffles, *The History of Java*, Oxford University Press: Singapore 1988; first published in two volumes by Black, Parbury & Allen, and John Murray: London 1817

Anthony Reid, *Southeast Asia in the Age of Commerce 1450-1680: The Lands below the Winds*, Yale University Press: New Haven 1988

James Rush, editor, *Java: A Traveller's Anthology*, Oxford University Press: Kuala Lumpur 1996

Gunawan Tjahjono, *Cosmos, Center and Duality in Javanese Architectural Tradition: The Symbolic Dimensions of House Shapes in Kota Gede and Surroundings*, dissertation submitted for PhD in Architecture, University of California: Berkeley 1989

Jan Veenendaal, *Furniture from Indonesia, Sri Lanka and India during the Dutch Period*, Foundation Volkenkundig Museum Nusantara: Delft 1985

Roxana Waterson, *The Living House: An Anthropology of Architecture in South-East Asia*, Oxford University Press: Singapore 1990

Augusta de Wit, *Java: Facts and Fancies*, first published by W.P. van Stockum: The Hague 1912; reissued by Oxford University Press: Singapore 1987

index

Page numbers in **bold** refer to illustrations.

A
Aalbers, A.F., 103, 137
ancestral portraits, **159**
ani-ani (tiny hand knife), 20, **200**
antique, **146**, **173**
  silver and ivory, **161**
Anwar, Chairul, 24
Apotik Sputnik, **138**, **139**
arches   see gateways
Ardyanto, **190**, **191**, **193**
Ardyanto house, **192-193**
art deco, 23, 25, 62, 102, 103, 108, **113**, **129**, **130**, **131**, **132**
art nouveau, 102
  stained-glass decoration, **96-97**
  -inspired design, **68**, **122**, **206**
  -styled furniture, **178–179**, **206**
Austronesian, 20
  heritage, **16**
  house, 20, 32
  migrations, 16
  prehistoric peoples of the *nusantara*, 18
  roots, 21
  structural principles, 104

B
Balai Udang (Shrimp Hall—officially Town Hall of Cirebon), 135
bamboo, **15**, 32, 102, **184**
  chick blinds, **170-171**
  incised, **182-183**
  walls, **17**
Bandung Technical College, **126**, **127**
Bangsal Trajumas pavilion, **82**
batik, 14, 17, 20, 72, 103, 143, 144, **150**, **184**, **190**
  bedspread made of Madurese *batik*, **176**
  from Central Java, **163**
  East Javanese indigo, **168**
  kawung (a pattern), **150**
  -making, **52**
  on silk, **195**
  studio, **153**
Beaux-Arts decoration, **97**
becak (passenger tricycle), **99**
bed, **110**
  18th-century, **176**
  Chinese-influenced, **202**
  day, **200**
  four-poster, **162-163**, **166-167**, **181**, **203**
  Madurese carved, **184**
bench, **144**, **168**
  East Javanese village type, **186**
  roadside, **23**
  village, **205**
Bin House, 195
bolsters, 33
Borobudur, 14, **15**, 21, 25, 32, **33**
  temple in, 18, 145
Bowie house, 145
bowls
  lacquered, **181**
  serving, **144**
brick, **34**
  house construction, 38
  gateways, **68**
  temples, 35
  Hindu-styled brick tower, **120**
bronze, **160**, **161**, **173**
Brotosisworo, Dra. S, 138
Buddha
  of Mendut, 33
  statues, 15
  Buddhism, 14
bupati (regents), 23

C
cabinet
  work, **115**
  makers, **203**
  also see *lemari*
Café Batavia, **108**
Candi Tegawangi, 34
candle stands, **148**
cane, 33
carving, **59**
  doors or wall panels, **65**
  gilded, **181**
  of Majapahit, **160**
  screens, **186**
  early-18th century, **202**
  wooden panels and screens, **203**
chairs, 200
  art-nouveau, **178-179**

armchair, 19th-century, **204**, **205**
  becak-style, **206**
  burgomaster's, **202**
  cowboy, **188**
  Empire, **78**, **202**
  Jepara, **77**
  kursi gobang (reclining chair), **146**
  Raffles, 23, 25, **72**, **77**, 144, 204
  Sheraton's, 77
  VOC, **154**, **160**
chest, **202**
  Madurese, **176**
  vanity, **201**
  wedding, **168**, **200**
Chinese 35
  community, 203
  dragon jar, **79**
  influence, **28**
  porcelain, **191**
  rice jar, **195**
  woodcarving, **114**
City Hall, Jakarta, **76**
Coen, Jan Pieterszoon, 39
colonialism, 72
  colonial leisure, **77**
  colonial prints and paintings of Bogor, 145
column, **95**
  European-inspired, 35
  central, **200**
  capital and pillar base, **54**, **201**
  Corinthian, **80**
  Tuscan order, **74**, **76**, **95**
Confucius, 14
copperware, **168**
Couperus, Louis, 74, 75

D
Daendels, 23, 75
Damais, Asmoro, 184
Delft Technological High School, 103
Dewi Sri (deity of rice and fertility), 20, 38, **200**
  Raden Sadono (Dewi Sri's male companion), 38, **201**
de Werde, H.P.A., 81
de Wit, Augusta, 72,74,143
door, 38, **64**, **65**, **118-119**
  screen, **148**
  also see Kudus doors, *pintu angin*

E/F
emperan (semi-veranda), 38, **61**
Empire chair, **206**
Empire-inspired chair, **78**
Ethical Policy, 23, 102

Fatabillab Museum, **39**
Fatmawati, 157
feng-shui, 143
furniture making in Jepara, **28**

G
gateways, **24**, **28**, 69
Ganesha (Hindu God), **152**
Garland, Linda, 145
Ghijsels, F. J. L., 103, 105
glass
  coloured, **113**, **129**
  painting, **26-27**, 196
  stained, **114**, **124**
  windows inspired by Frank Lloyd Wright, **110**
  grilles, **111**, **197**

H
Hardjonegoro, Kyai Raden Temenggong, house, 143, **152**, **153**, **154**
Havelaar, Max, 74
heirlooms, **200**
Hotel
  Keprabon, Solo, **132**
  Majapahit (formerly Oranje Hotel of Surabaya), **106-107**
  Surabaya, Bandung, **128**, **137**
hotel stairway, **133**
house, 21
  1925 luxury villa in Yogyakarta, **105**
  1991 house in Jakarta, **186-187**
  contemporary, 142-197
  excavated in Trowulan, 34
  façades from Gresik, **113**
  in Jakarta, **38**, **180**
  in Malang, East Java, **110**, **111**
  in Yogyakarta, **114**
  of the governor of West Java, **76**
  pre-war, **104**
  Sundanese, **15**
  East Java and Pasisir traditional, **65**
  Javanese traditional, 37, **52-53**, **116**

I/J
Ibrahim house, **142**, 145, **146-147**, **148**, **149**, **150**, **151**, **196**, **197**
Indo-European
  house, **19**
  hybrid, 25, 73
  pattern, **95**
Institute of Technology Bandung, (ITB), 104
Islam, 14, 21, 34, **40**, **118**
  reformist, 24

Jakarta History Museum, 202, 204

K
Karsten, Thomas, 87, 103, 104
  renovation of the Mangkunegaran palace, **88**
Kasepuhan Palace of Cirebon, **48**
Kartini, Raden Adjeng, 23
  house she grew up in, **90-91**
keris, 14
  holders, **200**
kobrongan (altar or shrine canopies), **157**, **158**, **166-167**, **202**
Kota Gede, 39, 61
kratons
  Kraton Kanoman, 35, **46**, **47**
  Kraton Kasepuhan, 35, **54-55**
  Kraton of Sultan Hamengkubuwono, **92-93**
  Kraton of Sumenep, **59**
  Kraton Yogya, Srimanganti Courtyard, **82**, **83**
  Kratons of Solo and Yogyakarta, 35
  Mangkunegaran Kraton in Solo, 104
Kudus
  door, **28**, **65**, 145
  tumpang sari, **190**
Kumara, Josephine, 195
Kussudiardjo house, **182-183**

L
lamp
  14th-century, **32**
  art-nouveau, **191**
  kerosene, **206**
  Memphis style, **191**
  oil, **201**
landscape, **10-11**, 9
lemari (cabinet), 144, **159**, **177**, **204**
limasan (roof type), 37
  pattern, 74
  roof ridges, **76**
loro blonyo, 38, **155**, **193**
  figures, **201**
  pair, **159**
  set, **157**
lotus, 35, **66-67**
Luytens, Sir Edwin, 196

M
Maclaine-Pont, Henri, 102, 103, 104, 126, 127
Majapahit
  gateway, **28**
  influence, 34
  legacy of, 48
  pattern, **29**
  styles, **161**
  -style tuff bust, **163**
  temples, **32**, 34
  tuff, **151**
Mangkunegaran palace, **88-89**, 104
Martaban jar (dragon jar), **197**
masks, **181**
mats, 33
Mesjid Sunan Giri shrine, **45**
Ming Dynasty, 34
  plates, **150**
modernism, 102-147
mosque, **26**
  at Mantingan, **40-41**, 186
  in Demak, 34, 35, **41**
  Menara Kudus, 35, **42**, **43**, **120**
mosquito nets, 75
motifs, **34**, **35**, **121**, 135, 158, **186-187**
Mpu Prapanca (holy man), 21
Mt. Merapi, **14**, 15, 17, 32
murals, **192-193**
musical instruments, **169**

N
naga (water dragon), **59**
Nagarakertagama (literary work), 21, 33
Naipaul, V.S., 16

Napoleon, 23
nation building, 24
neoclassical
  architecture, **18**, **142**
  emergence of, 75
  furniture   see chairs - Raffles
  impact of style in Java, **77**
  inspiration, **177**
  style, 25, **81**
  trends, 75
  villa, 25
Niagara hotel, **122**, **123**
nusantara (Greater Sunda), 15, 21, 104, 126, 127
Nyai Loro Kidul (the goddess of the Southern Sea), 38

O/P
omah (house proper), 38
Onghokam house, **178-179**
Ostenrijk house, 144, **186**

palm, **78**
  fibres, 33
  -leaf wrapping for *ketupat* rice cakes, **150**
Pasisir, 17, 18, 201
  port, 22
  street scenes from, **22**
pendopo (pavilion), **6-7**, 20, 35, **36**, **37**, 38, **46**, **47**, **54**, **116**, **117**, **143**, 144, 145, **153**, **166**, **176**
  in Solo, **57**, **174-175**
  Pendopo Agung of the Mangkunegaran, **86-87**
pici, **99**
pintu angin, (swinging doors), **113**, **114**
plates, **144**
Ponder, Harriet, 75
porcelain, 49, 69
Prambanan temple, **8-9**, reliefs, **32**

R
Raffles, Sir Stamford, 6, 15, 16, 23, 73
  bench, **177**
  brief rule, **77**
  chair   see chairs
  History of Java, publication, 23
Ramayana, 6, 21
Rappard, J.C., 73
rattan, 25, 32, 75, **77**, **113**
  caning, 204, 206
  chairs   see chairs
  mats, **200**
Regency
  design, **182**, 204
  -inspired village benches, **178**
  pedestal table, **166**
  settee design, **204**
  styles, **72**
religious
  school, **17**, **117**, **118-119**
  subjects, **26-27**
Renaissance style, **81**
rice, 16, 19, 20
  goddess   see Dewi Sri
  -growing plains, 17
  cultivation, 18
roof, **16**, **36**, **37**, 38, **42**, **43**, **54**, 69, 104, **105**, **116**, **178**
  also see *limasan*

S
sarongs, 72
Savoy Homann hotel, **136**, **137**
Schoemaker, C.P. Wolff, 103, 135
screen, **202**
  classic Jepara, **161**
  Gothic-revival folding, **206**
seals of the council members, 202
Semarangan, 206
  furniture, 102
  style, 105
Semar Tinandu pavilion, **48**
senthong (extended altar of three small rooms), 20, 38, **63**, 74, **157**
serambi (porch), **120**
Sheraton, Thomas, **77**
Soeharnoko apartment, 144, **160**
Soekarnoputra house, **156-157**
Soeharto, 24
Soekarno, Indonesia's first president, 24, 104, 157
Soemaljo, Yulianto, 74
souvenir industry, **173**
spittoon, **151**, **195**
stone
  buildings, 32

medallions, 34, **40-41**
Subiyakto family house, 144, **164-165**, **166-167**
Sultan Agung, 22, 39
Sultan Anom 1, 46
Sunan Gunung Jati
  tomb, **49**
Sunan of Solo, portrait, **84**
Suparto
  painting by, **177**
Supriyadi house, 145, **174-5**, **176**, **177**

T
table, 200
  coffee, Chinese, **189**
  pedestal, **205**
  Victorian marbletopped, **110**, **205**
  meja lurak (desk of village head), **170-171**, **204**
tablewear, **151**
Tagore, Rabindranath, 14
Tangkuban Perahu volcano, 126
teak, 206
  forests of Tuban, 21
  wood, **173**, **196**
  Tectona grandis, 32
Teater Kecil, **78**
Teknologi Bandung (ITB), **127**
tempo doeloe (design sensibility of the 19th and early 20th centuries), 24, 25, 72, 97, 72-99, 104
terracotta, **151**, **168**, **173**
  floor tiles, **78**
  plumbing, 34
  roof ridge tiles, **69**
textile
  heritage, 20
  makers, 20
  ikat, **176**
  wrapped, 33
The Toko Oen, **109**
Thornet bentwood rocker, **115**
Tirta, Iwan, 144, 158
Tirta house, **159**
tombs, 49
  Sunan Giri, **45**, **50**
  of the nine saints of Javanese Islam   see *wali sanga*
  Madurese tombstones, **59**
tumpang sari (ceiling of stepped timbers), 37, **54**, 57, 62
  carving, **174**
two lions of Fu, **111**

V
Van Pers, A., 74
Venetian and Moorish
  architecture, 142
  references, 145
Villa Isola, **135**
voorgalerij (veranda), 74, 177
  dining area, **170**
  furniture, **77**

W
wali sanga (the Nine Saints of Islam), 34, 49
  shrines of, 50
  also see Mesjid Sunan Gresik, Sunan Gunung Jati
Waringin (Banyan trees), 35
water gardens, **66-67**
wayang, 38
  characters from, 196
  clowns, **26-27**
  golek puppets, **181**
  kulit, **201**
weapons, **200**
Werkestatte, Weiner, 113
well, **67**
Westmaas, W., 81
Widodo house, **173**
wood
  carved plaques, **200**
  carving, **28-29**, 35
    Chinese influence, **28-29**
  jati (noble wood), **32**
  working in Jepara, **28**
  furniture and utensils from villages in East Java, **144**
  settee, **195**
wrought-iron
  brackets, **94**
  grilles, **111**
  railings, **98**